£8.99

hampsteadtheatre

WY**PLAY
HOUSE**

hampsteadtheatre and West Yorkshire Playhouse
present

fast labour

by Steve Waters

hampsteadtheatre and West Yorkshire Playhouse present

fast labour

by **Steve Waters**

Cast (in order of appearance)

Alexei	**Roger Evans**
Grimmer	**Mark Jax**
Victor	**Craig Kelly**
Anita	**Kirsty Stuart**
Andrius	**Joseph Kloska**
Tanya	**Charlotte Lucas**

Creative Team

Director	**Ian Brown**
Designer	**Simon Daw**
Lighting Designer	**Mark Doubleday**
Sound Designer	**Mic Pool**
Video Designers	**Simon Daw** and **Mic Pool**
Dialect Coach	**Neil Swain**
Fight Director	**Kate Waters**
Casting Director	**Siobhan Bracke**
Assistant Director	**Justin Audibert**
Deputy Stage Manager	**Kim Lewis**

The sets, props, costumes and technical aspects of this production were created by the West Yorkshire Playhouse Production Departments.

Press Officer (for **hampstead**theatre)	**Becky Sayer** (020 7449 4151)
Press Officer (for West Yorkshire Playhouse)	**Paula Rabbit** (0113 213 7273)

hampsteadtheatre and West Yorkshire Playhouse would like to thank:

Carphone Warehouse for supplying mobile phones
Burts Chips
Revolution in Hockley, Nottingham
IKEA

Fast Labour was first performed at West Yorkshire Playhouse in the Courtyard theatre on 19 April 2008

cast and creative team

Steve Waters (Writer)
Theatre credits include: *English Journeys, After the Gods* (Hampstead Theatre); *Habitats* (Gate, London/Tron, Glasgow); *The Unthinkable* (Sheffield Theatres); *World Music* (Donmar Warehouse); *Out of Your Knowledge* (Eastern Anglian tour). Steve is currently under commission to the National Theatre. Television and radio credits include: *Safe House, The Family Project, The Moderniser*. Steve currently runs the MPhil(B) in Playwriting at the University of Birmingham.

Roger Evans (*Alexei*)
Theatre credits include: *Woyzeck* (St Anne's, New York/Gate, London); *Rose Bernd, Professor Bernhardi* (Oxford Stage Co/Arcola); *How Love is Spelt* (The Bush); *The King Stag* (Young Vic); *Art and Guff* (Soho/Sgript Cymru); *Everything Must Go* (Sherman); *Gas Station Angel, Scum & Civility, The Man Who Never Yet Saw Woman's Nakedness* (Royal Court, International Festival); *Crash* (tour). Television credits include: *Midsomer Murders, Goldplated, Ghostboat, Aberfan, Sea of Souls, Casualty, Doctors, Murphy's Law, Absolute Power, Nuts & Bolts, The Bench I & II, Bradford in My Dreams, Sleeping with the TV On, A Mind to Kill, Rhinoceros, Syth, Crime Traveller, The Bill, Wonderful You*. Film credits include: *Gullible's Travels, Daddy's Girl, Atonement, All or Nothing, Human Traffic, Suckerfish*.

Mark Jax (*Grimmer*)
Theatre credits include: *Rough Crossings* (West Yorkshire Playhouse/Birmingham Rep/Liverpool Everyman/Lyric Hammersmith); *Mirror for Princes* (Barbican/Tour); *Jamaica Inn, Barbarians, The Norman Conquests* (Salisbury Playhouse); *Season's Greetings* (Mill at Sonning); *Prophet in Exile* (Chelsea Centre); *Laughter on the 23rd Floor* (Queen's West End/tour); *Mansfield Park* (Chichester Festival Theatre); *Way of the World, Macbeth, Tenant of Wildfell Hall, Peter Pan, Atheist's Tragedy, Romeo and Juliet, Rope, Women Beware Women* (Birmingham Rep); *Romeo and Juliet, Mansfield Park* (Sheffield Crucible); *The Devils* (Clywd Theatr Cymru); *Two Planks and a Passion* (Northcott Exeter); *When We Are Married* (WYP); *A Christmas Carol* (Young Vic); *Strange Kind of Animal, Pravda, The Government Inspector, The Futurists* (National Theatre); *The Dresser, Chorus of Disapproval, The Westwoods and I, Bricks and Mortars, The Linden Tree* (Stephen Joseph); *A Midsummer Night's Dream* (Theatre Royal Plymouth). Television credits include: *Marco Polo, Frankenstein, Doctors, Casualty, The Vice IV, The Bill, In the Beginning, Mary & Jesus, Merlin, Family Affairs, The Two of Us, A View from the Bridge, The Road to 1984, Most Dangerous Man in the World, Not a Penny More, Not a Penny Less, Shake Hands Forever, The Perfect Match, Grange Hill, Picture of Woman, Wuffer, Tales of the Unexpected*. Film credits include: *Stealing Heaven, Living Doll*.

Craig Kelly (*Victor*)
Craig trained at Drama Centre, London. Theatre credits include: *Helpless* (Donmar Warehouse); *The Fastest Clock in the Universe* (Bolton Octagon); *Song of an Honorary Soulman* (Shaw); *Babies* (National Theatre Studio); *The Wasp Factory* (Citizens', Glasgow). Television credits include: *Afterlife 2*, *Dalziel and Pascoe*, *Hotel Babylon*, *Totally Frank*, *Silent Witness*, *Waking the Dead*, *Helen of Troy*, *Clocking Off*, *Having it Off*, *'Love Gods'/Slices of Strange*, *The Grimleys III*, *Queer as Folk I & II*, *Children of the New Forest*, *Casualty*, *A Touch of Frost*, *The Young Indiana Jones Chronicles*, *Ellington*, *The Good Guys*, *Running Late*. Film credits include: *Are You Ready for Love*, *Oh Marbella!*, *Three Blind Mice*, *Silent Cry*, *Undertaker's Paradise*, *Killing Joe*, *Wing Commander*, *Titanic*, *When Saturday Comes*, *Young Americans*.

Joseph Kloska (*Andrius*)
Joseph trained at RADA. Theatre credits include: *The Vertical Hour* (Royal Court). Credits whilst training include: *The Life of Timon of Athens*, *Widows*, *Assassins*, *Sing Yer Heart Out for the Lads* (RADA); *Arcadia*, *Look Back in Anger*, *The Cherry Orchard*, *Cyrano de Bergarac*, *Julius Caesar* (University College, London); *Tales from Ovid* (Traumwand Project, Austria). Television credits include: *The Bill*, *Lark Rise to Candleford*. Film credits include: *Happy-Go-Lucky*, *Blooded*. Joseph was awarded the BBC Radio Carleton Hobbs Bursary Award 2006.

Charlotte Lucas (*Tanya*)
Charlotte trained at RADA. Theatre credits include: *World's End* (Trafalgar Studios); *Love Child* (Finborough); *Called to Account*, *Darfur – How Long is Never?*, *Fabulation* (Tricycle); *King Lear* (Creation Theatre Company); *Habeas Corpus* (Royal Theatre Northampton); *A Thought in Three Parts* (BAC); *Sharp Relief*, *Fen* (Salisbury Playhouse). Television credits include: *Midsomer Murders*, *The Bill*, *Judge John Deed*, *Holby City*, *Down to Earth*, *EastEnders*, *Adventure Inc.*, *Bad Girls*. Film credits include: *Last Chance Harvey*, *These Foolish Things*, *Oh Marbella!*.

Kirsty Stuart (*Anita*)
Kirsty trained at Drama Centre, London. *Fast Labour* marks her theatre debut. Credits whilst training include: *Mary Stuart*, *From Mayhew to Music Hall*, *Romeo and Juliet*, *Le Cid*, *Artists and Admirers*, *Pains of Youth*, *Fathers and Sons*. Television credits include: *Doctors*, *Sea of Souls III*, *The Marchioness*. Film credits include: *Closing the Ring*.

Ian Brown (Director)
Ian was appointed Artistic Director and Chief Executive of the West Yorkshire Playhouse in 2002, where he has directed *Macbeth*, *How Many Miles to Basra?* (Clarion Award 2007), *Foxes*, *Alice in Wonderland*, *Twelfth Night*, *The Lion, the Witch and the Wardrobe* (nominated for a TMA Award 2004), *Electricity*, *The Wind in the Willows*, *A Small Family Business*, *Pretending to be Me* (with Tom Courtenay), *Hamlet* (with Christopher Eccleston), *The Lady in the Van*, *Hijra*, *Eden End*, *Stepping Out*, *Broken Glass*, *The Comedy of Errors*, *Proposals*, *You'll Have Had Your Hole*, *Of Mice and Men*. Ian was also Associate Artistic Director of

the Playhouse for two years from 2000 to 2002. Other theatre credits include: *Equus* (Beer Sheva Theatre, Israel); *Goodnight Children Everywhere* (Olivier Award for Best New Play); *Victoria* (RSC); *Five Kinds of Silence* (Out of the Blue Productions); *Strangers on a Train* (Colchester/Guildford/Richmond); *Babycakes* (Drill Hall); *Fool for Love* (Donmar Warehouse); *Widows* (Traverse, Edinburgh); *Steaming* (Piccadilly); *Nabokov's Gloves* (Hampstead); *Killing Rasputin* (Bridewell); the original production of *Trainspotting* (Citizens', Glasgow/The Bush, London). From 1988 to 1999 Ian was Artistic Director and Chief Executive of the Traverse Theatre, Edinburgh. Productions included: *Reader, The Collection, Unidentified Human Remains and the True Nature of Love, Poor Super Man* (Evening Standard Award), *Ines de Castro, Light in the Village, Moscow Stations* (with Tom Courtenay – Evening Standard Award, Best Actor), *Hanging the President* (Fringe First Award), *The Bench, Hardie and Baird, Bondagers* (by Sue Glover, Scotland on Sunday Award and transfer to Donmar Warehouse/World Stage Festival, Toronto), *Shining Souls*. In 1999 Ian was awarded a Scotsman Fringe First and a Herald Angel Award for his work at the Traverse. Ian was also Artistic Director of TAG Theatre Company, Citizens' Theatre, for five years, where productions included: *Othello, A Midsummer Night's Dream, As You Like It, Romeo and Juliet, Hard Times, Can't Pay? Won't Pay!, Great Expectations* (Spirit of Mayfest Award). Before directing, Ian trained as a teacher and taught in a London comprehensive school. He became a community arts worker at the Cockpit Theatre in London and ran the Cockpit Youth Theatre. In 1982 he got his first professional job in theatre at the Theatre Royal, Stratford East, where he became Associate Director.

Simon Daw (Designer and Video Designer)
Theatre credits include: *Triple Bill: Baby Girl/DNA/The Miracle, The Enchantment* (National Theatre); *Elling* (Trafalgar Studios/The Bush); *French Without Tears* (English Touring Theatre); *Not the Love I Cry For* (Arcola); *Kebab*, Young Writers Festival 2002 (Royal Court); *Aladdin* (Bristol Old Vic); *Jackets* (Young Vic/Theatre503); *The Bodies* (Live Theatre); *Rutherford and Son* (Royal Exchange); *Tall Phoenix* (Belgrade); *Romeo and Juliet* (RSC); *Adam and Eve* (TPT, Tokyo); *Astronaut* (Theatre O/Barbican Pit/tour); *The Changeling* (National Theatre Studio); *Rafts and Dreams, Across Oka* (Royal Exchange Studio); *Relatively Speaking, The Witches, Everyman, Habeas Corpus* (Northampton); *Under the Curse, Tragedy: A Tragedy* (Gate, London); *Touched* (RSAMD); *The Singing Group, Exclude Me* (Chelsea); *Fragile Land* (Hampstead); *The Arbitrary Adventures of an Accidental Terrorist* (NYT/Lyric Hammersmith Studio); *Kes* (NYT/Lyric Hammersmith). Dance credits includes: *Bloom* (Rambert); *The Stepfather* (CandoCo Dance Company). Opera credits includes: *Fidelio* (Scottish Opera).
Installation/performance commissions include: *Wavestructures* (Aldeburgh Festival/online); *Hopefully it means nothing...* (Aldeburgh Festival/National Theatre); *New Town* (site specific & Arches, Glasgow); *Sea House* (Aldeburgh Festival).

Mark Doubleday (Lighting Designer)

Mark trained at the London Academy of Music and Dramatic Art where he won the Richard Pilbrow Prize. Mark worked for a year and a half with London Contemporary Dance Theatre before getting his first position as Lighting Designer at the Redgrave Theatre, where he lit over fifty productions. Opera credits include: *La Vie Parisienne* (D'Oyly Carte); *The Magic Flute, Così fan Tutte, Don Giovanni, Le Nozze di Figaro, Rigoletto, Les Contes d'Hoffman, La Bohème* (Stowe Opera); *Eugene Onegen* (MTL); *Die Fledermaus, Orlando Finto Pazzo, Shorts, Six-Pack, Family Matters* (Tête à Tête); *Falstaff* (RAM); *Le Nozze di Figaro* (Opera Zuid, Netherlands); *Hansel and Gretel* (Scottish Opera on tour); *Manon, Die Fledermaus* (English Touring Opera); *Ariadne auf Naxos* (Aldeburgh); *Le Torreador, Messalina, Amadigi, I Giardini della Storia* (Batignano, Italy); *La Fanciulla del West, Norma* (Opera Holland Park); *The Rape of Lucretia, Così fan Tutte* (RCM); *Nitro* (Royal Opera/BBC Linbury Theatre); *Lysistrata* (Houston Grand Opera, New York City Opera); *The Knot Garden* (Istituto di Musica di Montepulciano); *Odysseus Unwound* (Alexandra Palace); *Ariadne auf Naxos, Albert Herring* (Aldeburgh); *Tannhäuser* (Los Angeles Opera); *Mikado, Pirates of Penzance, Iolanthe* (Gielgud). London theatre credits include: *The Birds, The Colonel Bird* (Gate); *Retreat, Each Day Dies with Sleep, House Among the Stars, Lips Together, Teeth Apart* (Orange Tree); *The Danny Crowe Show, Elling* (The Bush); *On The Piste* (Garrick); *It Runs in the Family* (Playhouse); *Kit and the Widow* (Vaudeville and Ambassadors); *Gobbledegook* (Lyric Hammersmith); *Shadow of a Gunman* (Tricycle); *Easter* (Riverside Studios/Oxford Stage Company); *Out of Our Heads* (ATC); *Silverland, Not the Love I Cry For* (Arcola). Regional theatre credits include: *Love's Labour's Lost* (Shakespeare Theatre, Washington DC/RSC Stratford); *Behzti* (Birmingham Rep); *Tall Phoenix* (Belgrade, Coventry); *Broken Glass, How the Other Half Loves, The Deep Blue Sea, Get Ken Barlow* (Palace, Watford); *A Chorus of Disapproval, The Beggars Opera, Henry IV Parts I &II* (Bristol Old Vic); *Present Laughter, A Streetcar Named Desire, Misery* (Mercury, Colcester); *Forty Years On* (WYP). Mark has also lit in many other regional theatres including Nottingham Playhouse, York Theatre Royal, Wolsey Theatre Ipswich, Greenwich Theatre, Churchill Theatre Bromley, Queens Theatre Hornchurch, Liverpool Everyman and Playhouse, Nuffield Southampton, Northcott Exeter, Salisbury Playhouse. Future plans include: *Tannhäuser* (Teatro Real, Madrid); *La Cantatrice Chauve* (Athénée Théâtre Louis-Jouvet, Paris); *The Cumnor Affair* (Tête à Tête).

Mic Pool (Sound and Video Designer)

Mic has been involved in theatre for over thirty-one years. He has worked with numerous companies including the Lyric Hammersmith, the Royal Court Theatre, Ballet Rambert and the Royal Shakespeare Company. He has designed the sound for over 350 productions including more than 200 for West Yorkshire Playhouse, where he is currently Director of Creative Technology. He received a TMA Award in 1992 for Best Designer (Sound) for *Life is a Dream* and was nominated for both the Lucille Lortel and the Drama Desk Awards for Outstanding Sound Design 2001 for the New York production of *The Unexpected Man*. Mic was nominated for a 2007 Laurence Olivier Award for Best Sound Design for *The 39 Steps* at the Criterion Theatre. Recent sound design credits include: *The 39 Steps* (West End/UK tour/Broadway and worldwide); *The Hound of the Baskervilles* (Duchess/Yorkshire Playhouse); *Salonika, Beauty and the Beast, The Year of the Rat* (WYP). Video designs for theatre include: *Der Ring des Nibelungen* (Royal Opera House, Covent Garden); *Bad Girls –The Musical* (Garrick); *The Ethics of Progress* (Unlimited Theatre); *Don Quixote, The Lion, the Witch and the Wardrobe* (WYP).

Justin Audibert (Assistant Director)
Justin is currently Assistant Director in Residence at the West Yorkshire Playhouse and is studying for the Arts Council MFA in Theatre Directing at Birkbeck College, London. For West Yorkshire Playhouse, Justin has been Assistant Director on *The Grouch, Runaway Diamonds* (tour); *Beauty and the Beast*, Told By An Idiot's *Casanova* (UK tour/Lyric Hammersmith). He has also directed two short plays, *Ready Mades'* and *Trinity's Saint*, as part of Leeds Light Night '07 . Before coming to Leeds, he assisted Richard Beecham on *A Month In The Country*; Nick Tudor on *Nana* (both ArtsEd, London); Ken Christiansen on *A Torture Comedy* (Operating Theatre Company/Tristan Bates). Directing credits include: *Catfight, Please Don't Be Such a Brute* (Theatre503); *Seductions* (Komedia Roman Eagle Lodge); *Barcodes* (Camden People's Theatre); *Mojo* (Leeds Theatre Workshop and Stahl Theatre); *Rough for Theatre I* (Sheffield Theatre Workshop). Future directing work includes: co-directing an original piece of music theatre, *Armley: The Musical*, by Boff Whalley; assisting Rod Dixon on Red Ladder's 40th anniversary production, *Where's Vietnam?*, by Alice Nutter. Justin is seconded to West Yorkshire Playhouse from the MFA in Theatre Directing at Birkbeck University of London; as such it is fully professionally cast and staffed. The course is a new initiative to provide professionally based and professionally recognised training for directors. It has been established in collaboration with the theatre industry through the National Council for Drama Training and is supported by the Arts Council of England.

hampsteadtheatre

hampsteadtheatre is one of the UK's leading new-writing venues housed in a magnificent purpose-built state-of-the-art theatre – a company that is fast approaching its fiftieth year of operation.

hampsteadtheatre has a mission: to find, develop, and produce new plays to the highest possible standards, for as many people as we can encourage to see them. Its work is both national and international in its scope and ambition.

hampsteadtheatre exists to take risks and to discover the talent of the future. New writing is our passion. We consistently create the best conditions for writers to flourish and are rewarded with diverse award-winning and far-reaching plays.

The list of playwrights who had their early work produced at **hampstead**theatre who are now filling theatres all over the country and beyond include Mike Leigh, Michael Frayn, Brian Friel, Terry Johnson, Hanif Kureishi, Simon Block, Abi Morgan, Rona Munro, Tamsin Oglesby, Harold Pinter, Philip Ridley, Shelagh Stephenson, debbie tucker green, Crispin Whittell, Tamsin Oglesby and Roy Williams. Most recently it has produced award-winning plays by Nell Leyshon, Dennis Kelly and James Philips.

Each year the theatre invites the most exciting writers around to write for us. At least half of these playwrights will be emerging writers who are just hitting their stride – writers who we believe are on the brink of establishing themselves as important new voices. We also ask mid-career and mature playwrights to write for us on topics they are burning to explore.

hampsteadtheatre gratefully acknowledges the support of

  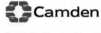

Funded by Camden Council

hampsteadtheatre's role as one of the finest new writing venues in London is made possible by the generous support of our Luminary members. We would like to thank the following individuals and companies for ensuring the future of our artistic and educational programmes.

our current luminaries are:

(as of March 2008)

Production Syndicate
Lloyd & Sarah Dorfman
Elizabeth & Daniel Peltz

Level 5
Janette & Danny Lesser
Eve & Ewan McGregor
Fiona & Gary Phillips
Solomon, Taylor & Shaw

Level 4
Leonard Eppel CBE &
 Barbara Eppel
Sir Richard Eyre
Sir Clement & Lady Jill Freud
Arnold Fulton
Midge & Simon Palley
Richard Peskin
Wendy & Peter Phillips
Anthony Simmonds
The Peter Wolff Theatre Trust

Level 3
Pauline & Daniel Auerbach
Dorothy & John Brook
David Cohen
The Sidney & Elizabeth
 Corob Foundation
Professor & Mrs C J Dickinson
David Dutton
George & Rosamund
 Fokschaner
Michael Frayn
Jacqueline & Michael Gee
Jay Harris
Rachele & John Harrison
Michael & Morven Heller
J Leon & Company Ltd
David & Wendy Meller
Brian & Hilary Pomeroy
Michael & Livia Prior
Paul & Claire Rayden
Sue & Anthony Rosner
David & Alexandra Scholey
Judy Williams

Level 2
Jenny Abramsky CBE
Bob Ainscow
Anonymous
Joan Bakewell CBE
The Ben-Levi Family
Judith & Shmuel Ben-Tovim
Karen Brown & John Blake
Bob & Jenni Buhr
Averil Burgess

Robin Cartwright
Frank Cass
Denis & Ronda Cassidy
Geraldine Caulfield
Jessica & Shimon Cohen
Conway Van Gelder Grant Ltd
R J Dormer
Robyn Durie
Peter English
Bernard Faber
Frankie de Freitas
Susan & Jeremy Freeman
Jacqueline & Jonathan
 Gestetner
MItchell Gitin
Richard Gladstone
Anthony & Claudia Goldstein
P & F Hackworth
Elaine & Peter Hallgarten
Robin & Inge Hyman
Paul Jenkins
Harold Joels
Norman & Doreen Joels
Reva & Robert Kahn
Patricia Karet
Sir Nicholas Kenyon
Tony Klug & Joanne Edelman
David Lanch
Jane Langer
Brian & Anne Lapping
Alasdair Liddell
Paul & Paula Marber
Julia & Julian Markson
Myra & Alec Marmot
Tom & Karen Mautner
Judith Mishon
Sandy & David Montague
Edna & Jerrold Moser
Nicholas Murphy
Trevor Phillips
Clare Rich
Rita & Anthony Rose
The Rubin Foundation
Henry & Esther Rudolf
 Charitable Trust
Jeoff Samson
Isabelle & Ivor Seddon
James Barrington Serjent
Dr Michael Spiro
Jonathan Stone
Clive Swift
Talbot Designs
Peter Tausig
Christopher Wade

Tom Wedgwood
Fraser & Sarah Whitehead
Hugh Whitemore & Rohan
 McCullouch
Dr Adrian Whiteson OBE &
 Mrs Myrna Whiteson MBE
Denise Winton
Della Worms &
 Fred Worms OBE
Stanley Wright

Level 1
David Adams
Martin Albu
Lord Archer
Graham & Michelle Barber
Eric & Jean Beecham
Michael & Leslie Bennett
Geoffrey & Lynn Bindman
Arline Blass
Alan Brodie Representation
Leonard Bull
Deborah Buzan
Felicity Coker
June Cowan
Mr & Mrs Michael David
Jose & David Dent
Ralph Emanuel
Eva & Desmond Feldman
Bobbie Ginswick
Desmond Goch
G C Goldman
Linda Goldman
Paul Harris
Simon Jones
Anne Katz
Lady Keegan
Roger & Yvette Kutchinsky
Siegi & Valerie
 Mandelbaum
David & Sandra Max
Raymond Mellor
Roger & Bridget Myddelton
Thomas Neumark
Rafe & Stacey Offer
Claudia Rosoux
Peter Roth QC
Marcus & Andrea Sarner
Michael & Luba Selzer
Lady Solti
Bonnie Tabatznik
Ann Vernau
Tim Watson
Derek Zissman

capital campaign supporters

hampsteadtheatre would like to thank the following donors who kindly contributed to the Capital Campaign, enabling us to build our fantastic new home.

Mr Robert Adams
Mr Robert Ainscow
Mrs Farah Alaghband
Mr W Aldwinckle
Mr Mark Allison
Anonymous
Mrs Klari Atkin
Mr William Atkins
Mr and Mrs Daniel and Pauline Auerbach
Mr David Aukin
Sir Alan Ayckbourn
Mr George Bailey
Mr Christopher Beard
Mr Eric Beecham
Mrs Lucy Ben-Levi
Mr Alan Bennett
Mr and Mrs Rab Bennetts
Mr Roger Berlind
Ms Vicky Biles
Mr Michael Blakemore
Mr Simon Block
Mr A Bloomfield
Mr John Bolton
Mr Peter Borender
Mr and Mrs Rob and Colleen Brand
Mr Matthew Broadbent
Mr Alan Brodie
Dr John and Dorothy Brook
Mr Leonard Bull
Mr and Mrs Paul and Ossie Burger
Ms Kathy Burke
Mr O Burstin
Ms Deborah Buzan
Mr Charles Caplin
Sir Trevor and Susan Chinn
Mr Martin Cliff
Mr Michael Codron
Mr and Mrs Denis Cohen
Dr David Cohen
Mr David Cornwell
Mr and Mrs Sidney and Elizabeth Corob
Mr and Mrs John Crosfield
Miss Nicci Crowther
Ms Hilary Dane
Mr and Mrs Ralph Davidson
Mr and Mrs Gerald Davidson
Mrs Deborah Davis
Mr Edwin Davison
Mr David Day
Ms Frankie de Freitas
Mr and Mrs David and Jose Dent
Professor Christopher and Elizabeth Dickinson

Sir Harry Djanogly
Ms Lindsay Duncan
Mr David Dutton
Mrs Myrtle Ellenbogen
Mr Michael Elwyn
Mr Tom Erhardt
Sir Richard Eyre
Mr Peter Falk
Ms Nina Finburgh
Mr and Mrs George and Rosamund Fokschaner
Ms Lisa Forrell
Mr N Forsyth
Mr Freddie Fox
Mr Michael Frayn
Mr Norman Freed
Mr Conrad Freedman
Mr and Mrs Robert and Elizabeth Freeman
Mr and Mrs Jeremy and Susan Freeman
Mr and Mrs Brian Friel
Mr Arnold Fulton
Mr and Mrs Michael and Jacqueline Gee
Mr and Mrs Jonathan and Jacqueline Gestetner
Mr Desmond Goch
Mr Anthony Goldstein
Mr Andrew Goodman
Ms Niki Gorick
Mrs Katerina Gould
Lord and Lady Grabiner
Mr and Mrs Jonathan Green
Mr and Mrs David Green
Mrs Susan Green
Mr Nicholas Greenstone
Mr Michael Gross
Mr and Mrs Paul Hackworth
Dr Peter and Elaine Hallgarten
Miss Susan Hampshire
Mr Christopher Hampton
Mr Laurence Harbottle
Sir David Hare
Lady Pamela Harlech
Mr Paul Harris
Mr John Harrison
Mr Howard Harrison
Mr Jonathan Harvey
Sir Maurice Hatter
Mr Marc Hauer
Dr Samuel Hauer
Mr and Mrs Michael and Morven Heller
Mr Philip Hobbs
Mr and Mrs Robin and Inge Hyman
Mr Nicholas Hytner

Ms Phoebe Isaacs
Mr Michael Israel
Professor Howard and Sandra Jacobs
Mr and Mrs Max Jacobs
Dr C Kaplanis
Mrs Patricia Karet
Baroness Helena Kennedy
Mrs Ann Kieran
Mr Jeremy King
Mr Peter Knight
Sir Eddie Kulukundis
Ms Belinda Lang
Mr and Mrs Edward Lee
Mrs Janette Lesser
Lady Diane Lever
Mr Daniel Levy
Mr Peter Levy
Sir Sydney and Lady Lipworth
Mrs Alyssa Lovegrove
Ms Sue MacGregor
Mr S Magee
Mr Fouad Malouf
Mr and Mrs Lee Manning
Mr and Mrs Thomas and Karen Mautner
Mr and Mrs David and Sandra Max
Mrs June McCall
Mr John McFadden
Mr Ewan McGregor
Mr and Mrs David Meller
Mr Raymond Mellor
Mr Anthony Minghella
Mr and Mrs David Mirvish
Mr and Mrs Mark Mishon
Mr and Mrs Edward and Diana Mocatta
Mr and Mrs Gary Monnickendam
Mrs and Mrs David and Sandra Montague
Mr Peter Morris
Mr and Mrs Ian Morrison
Mr Andrew Morton
Lady Sara Morton
Mr Gabriel Moss QC
Mr and Mrs Terence Mugliston
Mr and Mrs Roger and Bridget Myddelton
Mr Stewart Nash
Mr James Nederlander
Mr John Newbigin
Sir Trevor Nunn
Mr T Owen
Mr and Mrs Simon and Midge Palley
Mr Barrie Pearson

Mr Daniel Peltz
The Honorable Elizabeth Peltz
Mr Richard Peskin
Mr Gary Phillips
Mr Trevor Phillips
Mrs Gillian Phillips
Mr and Mrs Peter and Wendy
  Phillips
Mr Paul Phillips
Mr Tim Pigott-Smith
Mr Alan Plater
Mr Michael Platt
Mr and Mrs Brian and Hilary
  Pomeroy
Mr and Mrs Michael and
  Tamara Rabin
Mr D Randall
Mrs Janet Rapp
Mr and Mrs Paul and Claire
  Rayden
Mr Robert Reilly
Mr Dominic Ricketts
Mr Gillespie Robertson
Mr and Mrs Edward Roche
Mr D Rogers
Mr Gerald Ronson and Dame
  Gail Ronson DBE
Mr Benjamin Rose
Mr and Mrs Anthony and Sue
  Rosner
Mr Vernon Rosoux
Mrs Patricia Rothman
Mr Robert Rubin
Mr Michael Rudman
Mrs Esther Rudolf
Mrs Coral Samuel
Mr and Mrs Marcus and
  Andrea Sarner
Sir David and Lady Scholey
Mr James Barrington Serjent
Ms Louisa Service
Mr Cyril Shack
Mr and Mrs Peter Shalson
Mr and Mrs Gerry and Sue
  Sharp
Mr and Mrs Mike Sherwood
Mr Richard Shuttleworth
Mr and Mrs Jonathan and Lucy
  Silver
Mr and Mrs Anthony and
  Beverley Silverstone
Mr and Mrs Michael Simmons
Mr and Mrs Mark Simpson
Mr and Mrs Michael and Zsuzsi
  Slowe
Mr and Mrs Jeremy Smouha

Mr David Soskin
Dr Michael Spiro
Mr Nicholas Springer
Mr and Mrs Peter Sprinz
Mr Simon Stapely
Miss Imelda Staunton
Mr Bruce Steinberg and Ashley
  Dartnell
Ms Shelagh Stephenson
Mr Jonathan Stone
Sir Tom Stoppard
Mr David Tabatznik
Mr Paul Taiano
Mrs Valentine Thomas
Mr and Mrs Simon Tindall
Mr Fred Topliffe
Ms Jenny Topper
Mr and Mrs Barry Townsley
Mr Christopher Wade
Mr Vincent Wang
Mr Tom Webster
Mr Timothy West
Mrs L Westbury
Dr Adrian Whiteson
Mrs Judy Williams
Mr James Williams
Mr Richard Wilson
Mr Geoffrey Wilson
Mr Peter Wolff
Lady Ruth Wolfson
Mr and Mrs Fred and Della
  Worms
Mrs Marion Yass
Mr and Mrs Jeffrey and Fenella
  Young
Allied Irish Bank
Buro Four Project Services
Casarotto Ramsay and
  Associates
Charles Caplin & Co
Conway van Gelder Ltd
Ernest R Shaw Insurance
  Brokers
Friends of Theatre
Garfield Weston Foundation
Ham & Highgate Express
Hampstead Hill School
Hampstead Wells & Campden
  Trust
J Leon & Company Ltd
John Lyon's Charity
Kleinwort Benson Charitable
  Trust
Mercers' Company Charitable
  Trust
N M Rothschild & Sons Ltd

Nyman Libson Paul
Peters Fraser & Dunlop
RAC Plc
Richard Grand Foundation
Samuel French Ltd
The Acacia Charitable Trust
The Agency
The Allen Foundation for the
  Arts
The Andor Charitable Trust
The Archie Sherman
  Charitable Trust
The Arthur Andersen
  Foundation
The Barnett & Sylvia Shine No 2
  Charitable Trust
The British Land Company PLC
The Coutts Charitable Trust
The Dent Charitable Trust
The Dorset Foundation
The Drue Heinz Trust
The Duveen Trust
The Equity Trust Fund
The Esmee Fairbairn
  Foundation
The Follett Trust
The Garrick Charitable Trust
The Harold Hyam Wingate
  Foundation
The Hollick Family Trust
The John S Cohen Foundation
The Mackintosh Foundation
The Maurice Hatter
  Foundation
The Monument Trust
The Noel Coward Foundation
The Presidents Club
The Rayne Foundation
The Rose Foundation
The Royal Victoria Hall
  Foundation
The Sidney & Elizabeth Corob
  Charitable Trust
The Steel Charitable Trust
The Trusthouse Charitable
  Foundation
The Ury Trust
The Weinstock Fund
Wild Rose Trust

hampsteadtheatre would also like to thank the many generous
donors who we are unable to list individually.

thank you to the following for supporting our creativity:

Abbey Charitable Trust; Acacia Charitable Trust; The Andor Charitable Trust; Anglo American; Arimathea Charitable Trust; Arts & Business; Awards for All; Auerbach Trust Charity; Bank Leumi; The Basil Samuels Charitable Trust; Bennetts Associates; Big Lottery Fund; Blick Rothenberg; Bridge House Estates Trust Fund; The Chapman Charitable Trust; Swiss Cottage Area Partnership; The John S Cohen Foundation; Coutts Charitable Trust; Denton Wild Sapte Charitable Trust; D'Oyly Carte Charitable Trust; The Dorset Foundation; Duis Charitable Trust; The Eranda Foundation; The Ernest Cook Trust; European Association of Jewish Culture; Garrick Charitable Trust; Gerald Ronson Foundation; The Hampstead & Highgate Express; Hampstead, Wells & Campden Trust; Help a London Child; Harold Hyam Wingate Foundation; The Jack Petchey Foundation; Jacobs Charitable Trust; John Lyon's Charity Trust; Kennedy Leigh Charitable Trust; Local Network Fund; Mackintosh Foundation; Markson Pianos; Marriot Hotel, Regents Park; Milly Apthorp Charitable Trust; The Morel Trust: Nicole Farhi; The Noël Coward Foundation; Notes Productions Ltd; Parkheath Estates: The Paul Hamlyn Foundation; Pembertons Property Management; The Rayne Foundation; Reed Elsevier; Richard Reeves Foundation; Royal Victoria Hall Foundation; Salans; Samuel French; The Shoresh Foundation; Society for Theatre Research; Solomon Taylor Shaw: Sweet and Maxwell; Karl Sydow; Towry Law; The Vandervell Foundation; The Vintners' Company; World Jewish Relief; Charles Wolfson Foundation; Zurich Community Trust.

If you would like to become more closely involved, and would like to help us find the talent and the audiences of the future, please call Jon Opie on 020 7449 4174 or email development@hampsteadtheatre.com

hampsteadtheatre

WILL YOU?

Have you ever thought you could support
hampsteadtheatre by leaving a legacy?

hampsteadtheatre is a registered charity that exists
to present new writing for the stage. After years of
outstanding work, the theatre now has a home
to match its reputation for producing some of the most
exhilarating theatre in London.

In addition to producing ten full-scale productions
a year, we:

- Encourage diverse audiences to have a deeper
  understanding and appreciation of new plays in the
  theatre
- Support a successful integrated education
  programme that gives people, and young people in
  particular, the opportunity to participate in a wide
  range of writing and performance projects
- Read and respond to 1800 unsolicited scripts a year

hampsteadtheatre plays and will continue to play a
crucial role in the cultural life of its community.

If you leave a legacy to **hampstead**theatre this is free from tax.

For more information on leaving a legacy to
hampsteadtheatre, please get in touch with the Sarah Coop on
020 7449 4161 or email **sarahc@hampsteadtheatre.com**

WY PLAY HOUSE

Since opening in 1990, West Yorkshire Playhouse has established a reputation both nationally and internationally as one of Britain's most exciting and active producing theatres, which provides both a thriving focal point for the communities of West Yorkshire and theatre of the highest standard for audiences throughout the region and beyond.

The Playhouse regularly collaborates with other major regional producing theatres and companies. Past credits include: **The Bacchae** (2004) with Kneehigh Theatre; **The Wizard of Oz** (2005), **Alice in Wonderland**, **To Kill a Mockingbird** (2006), **The Lion, the Witch and the Wardrobe** (2007) and the forthcoming co-productions of **Hapgood** and **Peter Pan** with Birmingham Repertory Theatre Company; **Hedda Gabler** (2006) with Liverpool Everyman & Playhouse; **Wars of the Roses** (2006) with Northern Broadsides; **Flat Stanley** (2006) with Polka; **Ramayana** (2007) with Lyric Hammersmith and Bristol Old Vic; **Brief Encounter** (2007) with Birmingham Repertory Theatre Company and Kneehigh Theatre; **Casanova** (2007) with Told by an Idiot and Lyric Hammersmith.

West End transfers have included: **Ying Tong** (2004) to the New Ambassadors Theatre; **The Postman Always Rings Twice** (2005) to the Playhouse Theatre; the Olivier award-winning **The 39 Steps** (2005) which is currently playing at the Criterion Theatre, on Broadway and on UK tour; **The Hound of the Baskervilles** (2007) to the Duchess Theatre and, following its world premiere at the Playhouse in 2005, **Bad Girls – The Musical** (2007) to the Garrick Theatre.

www.wyp.org.uk

WY PLAY HOUSE

New Writing

The New Writing programme at West Yorkshire Playhouse aims to develop and produce some of the best new drama from regional, national and international writers. Since 2001 the programme has been expanded through collaboration with the BBC and has created a strong body of writers and new work for theatre, radio and television. This has included such successes as **Scuffer** (2006) written by Mark Catley, the **Northern Exposure** season of new plays which is now in its sixth successful year and **Writing the City**, a co-production with BBC Radio 3.

Internationally, the Playhouse co-produces and produces a diverse range of projects which has included **Don Quixote** (2007) by Colin Teevan and Pablo Ley and the **Janus** project which developed and presented sixteen new European plays in translation in 2006.

There are many ways to get involved in New Writing at the Playhouse, as a writer or an audience member. For writers, the best introduction is our script-reading service and guidelines for submitting scripts can be found on the website **www.wyp.org.uk**

We also showcase new work and plays in development. Coming up are **Born Abroad** the stories of the recently arrived in to West Yorkshire on 10 May and the showcase of work from our So You Want To Be A Writer? course on 6 June.

To be kept up to date about New Writing events and activities or added to the mailing list contact the **Box Office** on **0113 213 7700** or visit **www.wyp.org.uk** and sign up to the free ebulletin list.

For all other enquiries contact Alex Chisholm, Associate Director (Literary) on **alex.chisholm@wyp.org.uk**

FIRST FLOOR

2008 will see West Yorkshire Playhouse opening up a whole new theatre space, where young people from Leeds and the surrounding area can be creative and develop new skills. First Floor will be part of the neighbouring St Peter's Building, above the Wardrobe Bar where there will be activities after school, at weekends and in the holidays. Visual and performing arts activities will be offered on a drop-in basis and also on a more formal basis with accredited courses that will suit a range of learning styles.

West Yorkshire Playhouse has a seventeen-year history of delivering innovative and meaningful work within the local community. Through the development of a well-resourced arts space that is 'owned' by the young people of Leeds, First Floor will enable the Playhouse to continue to create pioneering projects and enrich the lives of hundreds of young people across the city and beyond.

Take a Second to Give to First Floor

The estimated cost of the refurbishment project is £578,000 and so far £300,000 has been raised from Arts Council England, various trusts and foundations and private donations.

You can help by making a donation in person, send us a cheque or by rounding-up the cost of your tickets when booking with Box Office or online at **www.wyp.org.uk**

Thanks

West Yorkshire Playhouse receives funding from

First Floor Supporters

LOTTERY FUNDED

THE
LINBURY
TRUST

Production Sponsors

BRUNTWOOD

The Lion, the Witch
and the Wardrobe

Sponsors of Spark

 PROVIDENT FINANCIAL

Media Sponsors

YORKSHIRE
Evening Post

The Lion, the Witch
and the Wardrobe

Directors Club

Gold Members

EVANS
property group

leeds
metropolitan
university

YORKSHIRE POST
NEWSPAPERS LTD

 PROVIDENT FINANCIAL

Silver Members

Beaverbrooks

•

itv Yorkshire

Bronze Members

InBev UKLtd

•

Matthew Clark

Charitable Trusts

Audrey and Stanley Burton 1960 Trust

The Charles Brotherton Trust

Clothworkers' Foundation

Harewood Charitable Settlement

Harold Hyam Wingate Foundation

Kenneth Hargreaves Charitable Trust

If you would like to learn how your organisation can become involved with the
success of West Yorkshire Playhouse,
please contact the Development Department on 0113 213 7275

Jean Lucas Marketing Associate*
Kathy Webster and Ted Donovan
Archivists*

Paint Shop
Virginia Whiteley Head Scenic Artist

Performance Staff
Andy Charlesworth and Jon Murray
Firemen
Andrew Ashdown, Jen Aspinall, Daisy
Babbington, Lucy Barrie, Rachel
Blackeby, Alexandra Bradshaw, Lucy
Bradshaw, Andrew Bramma, Chandy
Chima, Megan Christie, Ben Dalby, Will
Dawson, Leigh Exley, Amy Fawdington,
Andrew Gilpin, Emma Goodway, Deb
Hargrave, Fiona Heseltine, Jenniffer
Hogg, Joanna Hutt, Susan Ioannou,
Laura Jarman, Rachel Kendall, Alexandra
Lavelle, Robert Long, Victoria Long,
Allan Mawson, Hayley Mort, Molly
Nicholson, Katie Powers, Serena
Rapisarda, Amanda Robinson,
Charandeep Sandhu, Hannah Sibai, Faye
Stephens, Daneill Whyles, Rebekah
Wilkes, Ruth Young, Pat Gornall, Rachel
Mann, Katie Walton, and Danielle Le
Cuirot Attendants*

Press
Rachel Coles Head of Press and PR*
Paula Rabbitt Senior Press Officer*
Jane Verity Press Officer

Production Electricians
Matt Young Chief Electrician
David Bennion-Pedley Deputy Chief
Electrician
Chris Alexander, Andrew Bolton and Paul
Halgarth Electricians

Production Management
Suzi Cubbage Production Manager
Eddie de Pledge Production Manager
Dickon Harold Head of Technical Design
Christine Alcock Production Administrator

Props Department
Chris Cully Head of Props
Sarah Barry Deputy Head of Props
Susie Cockram and Ben Parker Prop
Makers

Restaurant and Bar
Gary Barlow Hospitality Services Manager
Louise Poulter Kitchen Manager
Caroline Williams Chef Manager
Kirsty Crerar Chef de Partie
Linda Monaghan Commis Chef
Robert Cawood, Damian Jenkinson and
Peter Brown Kitchen Porters

Diane Kendall Restaurant Supervisor
Lee Dennell and Tam Sobeith Bar
Supervisors
Jade Gough, Kath Langton*, Esther
Lewis, Johnathan McGinlay, Kelly Baker,
Arron Kirk, Abigail Parkes and Mathew
Turner* Restaurant Assistants
Tracey Hodgetts, Elizabeth Carter, Amy
Pinder, Gareth Wilson, Sean Exley, David
Crozier, Mathew Gooch and Abbie
Johnson Bar Assistants*

Scenic Construction
Dickon Harold Acting Head of Workshop
Julian Hibbert and Ralph Tricker
Carpenter and Metal Worker
Kevin Cassidy, Nick Mulcahy and Abi
Emmett Additional Construction Staff

Security
Denis Bray Security Manager
Glenn Slowther Security Officer
Mayfair Security

Sound Department
Andrew Meadows Head of Sound
Martin Pickersgill Deputy Head of Sound
Mathew Angove Sound Technician

Technical Stage Management
Michael Cassidy Technical Stage Manager
Chris Harrison Deputy Technical Stage
Manager
Nidge Solly and Marc Walton Stage
Technicians
Dan Alcock, David Berrell, Matt de
Pledge, Matt Hooban and Darren
Kershaw Stage Crew

Theatre Operations
Jeni Chillingsworth House Manager
Jonathan Dean, Corinne Furness and
Tam Sobeih Duty Managers

Wardrobe Department
Stephen Snell Head of Wardrobe
Victoria Marzetti Deputy Head of
Wardrobe
Julie Ashworth Head Cutter
Nicole Martin Cutter
Alison Barrett Costume Prop Maker/Dyer
Victoria Harrison and Catherine Lowe
Wardrobe Assistants
Nicola Brown Wigs Supervisor
Catherine Newton Wardrobe
Maintenance/Head Dresser
Anne Marie Hewitt Costume Hire
Manager

*Denotes part-time

tried caza yet?

you are in for a tasty surprise!

Experience the taste of brilliant cooking at Caza. Our exclusive gourmet delights are prepared by highly trained chefs to exacting standards

Our menu is prepared from the finest selection of Italian & Mediterranean ingredients which are all put together from scratch to bring you the goodness of our tasty dishes. We pride ourselves in our honest food quality, excellent customer service and elegant yet Caza (homely) atmosphere.

Try our Sunday 2 course set lunch for £11.95 or 3 course for £13.95. We also have a weekday lunch special for £6.95. Available till 5.00pm.

caza
RISTORANTE

10% discount
when you mention
this offer

250 Finchley Road,
Hampstead, N
Tel: 020 7794

with any other offers

Opening Hours:
Mon - Sat: 11am to 12am
Sun: 12pm to 8pm

Parking available on bus lanes after 7pm
Pay & Display parking available on the road opposite the restaurant

Italian & Mediterranean

FAST LABOUR

Steve Waters

This play is dedicated to my parents,
Derek and Yvonne Waters,
and to economic migrants like them everywhere

Steve Waters would like to thank the following people for their assistance in developing this play:

Bridget Anderson, Jack Bradley, Ian Brown, David Carter, Alex Chisholm, Tony Clarke, D.I. Paul Cunningham, Lucy Davies, Olesya Khromeychuk, Felicity Lawrence, The Peggy Ramsay Foundation, Alex Orlov, Frances Poet, Don Pollard, Josie Rourke, Alex Sousa, Stepan Shakhno, Lionel Shefford and all the actors involved in workshopping the play.

The old lady thought it over. She saw that the transaction certainly seemed profitable, but it was something a little too novel and unusual. That made her fear the purchaser might cheat her in some way. After all, he had arrived goodness only knows from where and in the middle of the night too.

'Well, ma'am, is it a deal?'

'Really, sir, I've never had occasion before to sell dead peasants. Living ones I did dispose of once. Three years ago I let our parish priest have two girls for a hundred roubles each. And very grateful he was for them too. They've turned out to be fine workers. They can even weave table napkins.'

'Well, it's not a question of the living. I've nothing to do with them. I'm asking for the dead.'

Nikolai Gogol, *Dead Souls*

Characters

VICTOR, *late 30s, Ukrainian*
TANYA, *late 30s, his wife*
ANITA, *mid-20s, Scottish*
ANDRIUS, *late 20s, Lithuanian*
ALEXEI, *mid-40s, Russian*
GRIMMER, *50s, English*

Settings

Act One
A fish-processing factory in Scotland; Anita's flat; on the side of the A1; a farmhouse in Norfolk.

Act Two
A garden near Ely; a motorway service station; a rented house in King's Lynn.

Act Three
Victor's house in King's Lynn.

Note on dialogue

When two Russian-speaking characters are alone together, we assume they are speaking in Russian – and they speak in the actor's given voice; when a third non-Russian party is present they speak English unless specified.

This text went to press before the end of rehearsals and so may differ slightly from the play as performed.

ACT ONE

Scene One

A fish-processing factory in Scotland; winter. The changing rooms; lockers, a coffee machine, showers off left; sounds of machines and shopfloor off right. GRIMMER, *smoking, stands with* ALEXEI, *inspecting* VICTOR.

GRIMMER. Look at the state of that.

Looks like last night's kebab.

Smells like last week's chicken korma.

ALEXEI (*to* VICTOR). Strip *muzhik*.

Strip.

VICTOR *looks blank;* ALEXEI *shoves him;* VICTOR *starts to undress.*

GRIMMER. No spring chicken neither.

Said I wanted students.

ALEXEI. He work good.

GRIMMER. Look at his shoes. Jesus H.

In tatters. Did I ask for pikeys?

Can get cartloads of pikeys myself.

ALEXEI. Hard worker.

GRIMMER. Whole batch this rough? How many?

ALEXEI. Nine.

GRIMMER. They need fifteen.

ALEXEI. Only nine.

GRIMMER. They teach you boys numeracy?

Don't ask for business studies – they need fifteen, I promised fifteen – I'm proverbial for quality, Alexei, quality control, quality checks. Clean him up!

ALEXEI *bundles* VICTOR *off; wails from a clearly cold shower.*

They see me overextended, they go elsewhere; they go elsewhere, you go back where you came from.

ANITA *enters.*

ANITA. Can you not read, Mr Grimmer?

Non-smoking premises.

GRIMMER. Sure, sure, love – hygiene. Absolutely.

ANITA. Aye. We don't want wee kiddies catching E. coli.

He stubs it out.

GRIMMER. How we doing? Looking busy, everyone industrious, looking lovely.

ANITA. Oh aye, even better if you delivered on your pitch.

GRIMMER. We in a particular phase of the moon, today?

Second quarter, is it?

ANITA. *So* not funny. Okay, eight deadbeats, three of whom couldnae read the back of a fag packet that wasnae in Cyrillic script and one of whom in my view should be in A&E for second-degree burns –

GRIMMER. Sustained on your premises –

ANITA. – sustained on our premises 'cos she came here hotfoot from a ten-hour shift at NorFish –

GRIMMER. No, you know I don't allow moonlighting –

ANITA. – so tired out she didnae see the instructions on the cleansing vat –

GRIMMER. Let's not fall out, darling –

ANITA. – we have a duty of care to these people!

GRIMMER. I'll take her off your hands.

ANITA. Och, it's not a question –

GRIMMER. She's gone, off your hands, off your conscience –

VICTOR re-enters, wet, naked, with a hand-towel.

Anyway, here's number nine.

ANITA. Hey, will you cover yourself up? Jesus. You call that a towel? Get the guy a decent towel, that's a hand-towel.

She finds a better towel.

Do they not come with clothes, now?

GRIMMER. He'll be dandy in your standard gear.

ANITA. Okay, so now we have to dress 'em too now, that's a new low, dear God. Okay, okay –

Goes to a locker.

Here. Issue stuff, here.

Look at his back there. That bruising. Let me see that –

ALEXEI. He okay.

ANITA. This your first-aider? Serious contusion, that.

GRIMMER. Superficial. Looks more dramatic than it actually is.

ANITA. Presumably his stamp, National Insurance number, visa, is all in order?

GRIMMER. In the post.

ANITA. So, no papers, no clothes, no English –

GRIMMER. But on the upside he's got a very pleasant manner.

ANITA. I take it you know where he's from?

GRIMMER. Oh, we're ever so attentive to source.

(*To* ALEXEI.) Where's he from?

ALEXEI. East Europe.

ANITA. Could you not be a wee bit more specific?

GRIMMER. East of Ipswich, anyroad.

ANITA. Does he have a name or would that be pushing my luck? (*To* VICTOR.) D'you have a name?

VICTOR *and* ALEXEI. Victor.

GRIMMER. Victor. There you go.

ANITA. Victor. No, I can't take you, Victor, sorry. Sorry. But there it is.

She starts to go.

GRIMMER. Okay, okay fine. Fine. Get his stuff together, Alexei.

Lady says, 'No.' Five refrigerated trucks waiting in Goods Outwards; lady says, 'No thanks.'

Five competitor companies in a five-mile radius, five pallets of shellfish defrosting in the loading bays awaiting the tender offices of my people, all of whom, like Victor here, are gagging to work, still Ms Del Monte says, 'No.'

Is the gaffer in? Phil? Always go for a pint when he's in Lowestoft. Good sort. For a Scot.

GRIMMER *starts to go,* ALEXEI *after,* VICTOR *speaks.*

VICTOR. Want work. Work? Want work now.

ANITA. Three whole words.

GRIMMER. Four. Counting the name.

VICTOR. Want work.

ANITA. Sure you do, whole world does.

GRIMMER. How far's he come to get here, eh? Thousand mile?

ALEXEI. Two thousand.

GRIMMER. Two thousand mile to do a job you lot don't reckon's worth the bus fare. That's getting on your bike, alright, that's your work ethic, that's the calibre of person you're looking at. Two thousand mile. And for today, special offer, as he's on the premises, he comes gratis. Buy one get one free.

Pause.

ANITA. This is the last time.

GRIMMER. Good girl, good girl. You ever need another job, you know where I am – just don't chew my nuts off, alright? Only got the regulation two.

(*To* ALEXEI.) Call NorFish, tell them we're running late.

They go. VICTOR *and* ANITA *alone.*

ANITA. Okay, okay, you need overall, hairnet, gloves.

This your footwear? Christssake.

She picks up a mouldering training shoe in shreds.

That guy should equip you with working gear, you know. It's minus two on some of our lines.

I'm answerable to Health and Safety for you.

You getting anything I'm saying?

Not a fucking syllable.

Speaks into a mobile.

Shirley, hi, send, eh, Andrius is it, to the men's changing room.

Pause.

You'll want your complimentary coffee?

VICTOR *shrugs.* ANITA *goes to the coffee machine.*

Take it you'll have milk.

Give the guy milk, Anita. And sugar.

Beef you up a wee bit. State of you.

VICTOR *puts on the hairnet. It's too small.*

State of you!

She laughs. VICTOR *doesn't.* ANDRIUS *enters.*

Okay, Andrius, you're Russian, right?

ANDRIUS. Lithuanian.

ANITA. Yeah, but you speak Russian.

ANDRIUS. Lithuanian people forced to speak Russian until 1989.

ANITA. Whatever. Ask this guy how he got this bruising?

ANDRIUS. I am sorry?

ANITA. Bruising? On his back.

ANDRIUS (*in Russian*). She wants to know why you're damaged goods.

VICTOR (*in Russian*). I don't want to say.

ANDRIUS (*in Russian*). Make something up.

VICTOR (*in Russian*). I fell out a truck in Plovdiv.

ANDRIUS. He sustained injury in transit.

ANITA. Don't get bruising like that on British Airways. Even in cattle class. Where's his stuff, his luggage?

ANDRIUS (*in Russian*). She questions your mode of transportation.

She wonders why you don't have… possessions.

VICTOR (*in Russian*). Turkish fuckers robbed me in my sleep.

ANDRIUS (*in Russian*). Don't tell her that.

VICTOR (*in Russian*). No, okay, sure. Tell her – tell her I'm careless.

No. Tell her I want to work. Hard.

ANDRIUS. He wishes to inform you that he is ready for work.

Pause.

ANITA. Okay. Fabuloso.

So tell him we're a fish-processing concern, herring, mackerel, monkfish, he'll be mainly herring, he'll be topping and tailing, filleting, getting the wee pin-bones out – stress to him, if there's a single bone left in the fish, the supermarkets reject the whole batch, so stress that he takes great care – sorry, go on –

ANDRIUS (*in Russian*). You take bones out of fish.

You chop heads off fish and then tails.

Get all the bones out or they sack you.

ANITA. Y'done?

Main thing is he reports to his team leader, Shirley Brodie, line four, all the team leaders are in the orange suits, big lady with a perm –

ANDRIUS (*in Russian*). You work for an old bitch.

Curly hair. Hates foreigners.

ANITA. He gets forty-five minutes for lunch, including toilet break; and he's requested to keep to the left-hand area of the canteen and to only consume food purchased on the premises, and after lunch to scrub with the antibiotic soap for three minutes, top, under hand, between the fingers.

ANDRIUS (*in Russian*). Forget lunch.

Alexei drives us to the chip shop later.

Smoke on the loading bays.

Don't talk to the locals. Don't look at the women.

ANITA. Err, SeaFresh is an Equal Opportunities employer. I am Anita, I'm in charge of Human Resources and if you, Victor, experience any harassment, bullying or have any complaint or query, my door is always open.

ANDRIUS (*in Russian*). This lady is the closest thing to a human being in this building. Everything else is a cunt or a fish. Sometimes both at once.

VICTOR *laughs*.

ANITA. Why's he laughing now?

ANDRIUS. I do not know. You must ask him.

ANITA. What's the joke, fella?

VICTOR *waves her away; his laughter is hard to control; he signals to his hairnet*. ANITA *laughs*.

Yeah, you do look a great big Jessie, yeah.

Take him to Shirley.

ANDRIUS. For sure.

As they go, VICTOR *turns and holds* ANITA*'s hands.*

VICTOR. Thank you, Anita.

ANITA. Sorry?

VICTOR. Thank you – Anita.

He indicates the coffee cup.

ANITA. Just a wee cup of coffee, Victor.

VICTOR *and* ANDRIUS *go.*

Scene Two

ANITA*'s flat; spring. She's dressed up.* VICTOR*'s in work clothes and a wet kagool. On the floor are box files, CDs, a sense of disorder.*

ANITA. See the North Sea from here. The sea? See?

VICTOR *nods.*

Your basic beach, sand and that. Actually quite a nice beach. Almost pretty. 'Pretty'? In summer.

Mind you, summer can be pretty elusive up here.

Now, look at you in your kaggie.

Get these things off, they're soakin', there.

He takes off his coat; she takes it offstage. He looks around.

(*Off.*) You near a sea? Back home?

What's your sea?

VICTOR. Sea?

She re-enters.

ANITA. Caspian Sea? Black Sea?

VICTOR. Black Sea, yes. You go Black Sea?

ANITA. Black Sea? No, no.

Looked it up on Google Map.

VICTOR. Not understand.

Pause.

ANITA. No. You holiday there? The Black Sea? Swim?

VICTOR. When – boy. Err. Err. Boys. Err – fires… err – fish, err, walking.

He marches, sings 'Komsomol' marching song.

ANITA. Oh, okay, like the Scouts and that? Like Scout, err, camp?

VICTOR. Not understand.

ANITA. Cub Scouts? Uniforms and that.

I was a Beaver myself. For about a week.

Pause.

VICTOR. Miss Strang.

ANITA. Call me Anita. Here or there. We're very informal as you may have noticed.

VICTOR. Anita. Why ask me – here?

ANITA. Oh. Well, why not?

There's nothing against it. In the rules.

If you were on the books, mebbe. I mean, permanently.

But you're not.

Pause.

Place is a tip; some Beaver I am.

Living on your tod you let things slide. Post is all Freepost; recycling I never get round to, stack it and chuck it. Shocking.

Do you smoke?

VICTOR. Smoke? Yes.

ANITA. That's cool. Here, have one of mine. Here. I'm endeavouring to quit. With limited success.

She gives him a cigarette; she lights hers and then his. They smoke in silence.

Hey. Do me a massive favour, have the packet.

VICTOR. No, no.

ANITA. Seriously. It was an impulse-buy in Mace.

He takes it. Pockets it.

VICTOR. Thank you.

ANITA. Always thanking me. Just a packet of fags, right!

Pause.

I'm talking too much.

Oh, music, music. Do you like music and stuff?

VICTOR. Music? Of course.

ANITA. Right. I like R'n'B. D'you like that, d'you get R'n'B?

VICTOR. R and B, yes yes. Heavy rock. Very good.

ANITA. Heavy rock?

VICTOR. Err, Lid Zip. Lid Zip.

ANITA. No. They Ukrainian?

VICTOR. No, no. English, British. Lid Zip.

ANITA. Don't sound very English.

VICTOR. 'Stairway Heaven'.

ANITA. Did it chart?

VICTOR. Err. 'Whole Lot Love'. 'Got a whole lot love, got a whole lot love…' Very famous, world famous.

ANITA. Oh, Led Zeppelin!

VICTOR. Yes, Lid Zip.

ANITA. My dad loves those guys.

Pause.

Don't reckon you'll like my CDs.

Pause.

Grimmer looking after you okay, then?

VICTOR. Mr Grimmer. Good.

Pause.

ANITA. I'm not fond of Davies, you know, my boss, Mr Davies, but he's been okay to me. Didn't much like implementing the new contracts, but hey, there's worse down the road, this is business. Didn't much like getting called a scab by the slags I was at school with, to be honest, most of them never liked me anyway, figured I was, you know, a snob or something, 'cos I didnae get knocked up at sixteen, 'cos I read the *Daily Mail* rather than *Heat* – but hey, it's all a job, all within the law, so okay.

But now, you guys, you know –

VICTOR. Not understand.

ANITA. No. Course not. But he treats you – okay?

VICTOR. No problem. Grimmer good.

ANITA. You don't trust me, do you?

VICTOR. 'Trust'?

ANITA. See, I've been watching the guy – he's a lech for one; I mean, Davies eyes you up but he's too scared of his wife to go the extra mile, but Grimmer's got eyes that –

VICTOR. All good, good. Now I go, go, goodnight.

ANITA. No, sit down, sit down, I'm cooking, right – and you're
hungry, right. Right?

VICTOR. Yes.

ANITA. And you eat pizza with anchovies and pineapple and shit?

VICTOR. Yes like good.

ANITA. I mean, you're so skinny. Look hungry all the time.
Entire time you been with us you look famished. Never seen
you in the canteen.

VICTOR. No.

ANITA. Tell you for nothing, your shifts are mental. Dangerous.

You don't have to work the double shift, whatever Dickhead
Davies says. We have regulations to protect you, the
Working Time Directive.

VICTOR. Wish to work.

ANITA. Yeah, I know, I see that. You take care though.

VICTOR. Happy to work. Life good here.

ANITA. You seen your contract, Victor?

VICTOR. What?

ANITA. A contract. Hang on. Okay, here goes.

She finds a bag, pulls a document from it.

I know it'll mean little to you, I know.

Contract. Payment – to you, well, any one of you, from
Davies to Grimmer. Look, here, look: actual wage is okay,
minimum wage, yeah, all the deductions those are the – the
whole works. I mean, it's not good money but it's not bad
money. So how much – how much of this do you get to see?
Victor? How much of this money d'you get to see? There,
hourly rate, hours worked, yeah. Tax code.

VICTOR *takes the contract, looks at it; tries to hand it back.*

No. You keep it. You keep hold of it. It's fine, yours.

I took a copy.

VICTOR. Trouble for you. No –

ANITA. Oh no. You see, this is my thing: tomorrow I am gone,
I am out of there. Fuck 'em. Resigned – by email!

Pretty cool, huh?

VICTOR. Gone?

ANITA. Aye. I've had it. Had enough of… seeing things –

He folds up the contract.

Okay, look at you, starved: get the man pizza, Anita.

VICTOR. It's good. To be here. In house.

ANITA. Just a wee flat.

She goes off.

(*Off.*) And you're up on windy watch hill, right?

VICTOR. Caravan.

ANITA (*off*). Pretty drafty.

VICTOR. No, not understand?

ANITA (*off*). Pretty, err, windy up there.

VICTOR. Yes. Cold.

She comes back in.

ANITA. Don't go back there. Tonight.

VICTOR. What? Bed, for me, friends, must go to…

ANITA. Don't go back, tonight, to your caravan.

VICTOR. Must go.

ANITA. No, stay here. Tomorrow, fine, tomorrow, okay, you
can go and talk to someone, you – go up the Citizens Advice
Bureau or something.

VICTOR. No, no. No.

ANITA. I mean, I could put you up a night or two.

Get you work elsewhere, get you placed, I mean, I can do that.

VICTOR. No.

ANITA. And I have the other room.

VICTOR. No.

ANITA. Davies phoned Immigration. Immigration.

Not 'cos he cares, oh no, he couldn't give a flying fuck about the law, oh no.

VICTOR. My money, no money.

ANITA. Well, he can't not pay you. You have your rights.

VICTOR. No.

ANITA. No, you do. As a worker.

VICTOR. No.

ANITA. Yes yes, if you're legal.

VICTOR. No no no.

Silence.

ANITA. Okay. You're not – yeah, well, I knew – that. Okay.

Pause.

Same difference, to me, Victor. Same difference.

But you go back tonight and you'll be gone by morning. They'll put you in a van, stick you on a plane and all of your efforts will be for nothing.

So, stay.

VICTOR. Tomorrow?

ANITA. Yeah. I know. Tomorrow's tomorrow. Stay. Tonight.

Pause.

VICTOR. Why me, Anita? Why not – others?

ANITA. Well. Can hardly fit the lot of you in here, can I?

They laugh.

VICTOR. Don't know me.

ANITA. Not seen the likes of you before. Work like a Trojan, always this great grin on your face. I – like you, like the look of you. God, that came out fast.

VICTOR. You talk me.

ANITA. Course I do. What am I? Course I talk to you.

VICTOR. You see me. First day. No… clothes.

ANITA. Oh, it's not that, jeeze, that was… a fine sight, that.

She laughs, so does he.

Probably breaking some code of practice.

But fuck it, fucking Davies, Grimmer, fucking sleazebags.

VICTOR. Sorry?

ANITA. This shouldnae happen to you.

You're a grown man. You work hard.

VICTOR. I do not give – over? Over?

ANITA. 'Give in.'

He writes this down.

VICTOR. I do not give in, Anita. I fight. Or now, give in, later, fight. Fight later, now, give in.

Suddenly VICTOR is weeping.

ANITA. Hey, hey. You… here – hey.

She touches him; he holds her hands.

It's okay, pet. You'll come good.

VICTOR. Good hand.

ANITA. Just a wee mitt.

He suddenly kisses her.

That's nice.

They kiss again.

That's lovely.

They lock into a kiss and it's messy.

Hang on. Wait up. Hang on a sec.

VICTOR. Sorry. Smell… nice.

ANITA. Get my breath back. Phew.

They laugh.

I don't make a habit of dragging lonely foreign guys back to my flat – You hitched? I mean, attached? I mean, is there a woman?

VICTOR. Sorry?

ANITA. No. You're a loner. Like me.

She moves in to him.

I like you, Victor. You're alive, yeah.

You're warm. Most of the blokes here.

Most of 'em. I'm not slagging them off.

They're mates, some of them. Been at school with 'em.

But they're unimaginative. They do what they're told.

They've been nowhere – I've been nowhere, who am I?

I just think it takes guts to be you, to up-sticks and – to do what you've done. Guts.

He goes to kiss her.

ANITA. Victor.

Pause.

VICTOR. I like you. You human being.

They kiss again, more messily, then fluently, then sexually. The sound of a ship horn.

Scene Three

On a road siding somewhere on the A1; the next day. VICTOR *seated, in shock,* ANDRIUS *battling with a map;* ALEXEI *off. It's early.*

ANDRIUS. English maps are crap. Blue, okay, blue, on any normal map, blue means water: rivers, canals, lakes. Blue's the universal symbol for water. Here, blue means road.

VICTOR. Motorway.

ANDRIUS. Correct. Which has three lanes?

VICTOR. Yes.

ANDRIUS. Yes, okay, but this motorway here, down here, is red.

VICTOR. Two lanes.

ANDRIUS. Yeah, okay, but look, now it's blue again. This map is total crap.

VICTOR heaves, stumbles off, is sick.

Yes and here it's blue. And here. 'A1(M)'. What the fuck is the 'A1(M)'?

VICTOR comes back on.

VICTOR. Look at my hands. Shaking.

ANDRIUS. Pretty minor scrape, by Alexei's standards.

VICTOR. Should have seatbelts, minimum.

ANDRIUS. Oh, right, seatbelts. Do cows generally get seat-belts? Think about it.

Sound of a large truck passing close.

VICTOR. We should get clear off the road.

ANDRIUS. I think it's fair to say we're well off the road.

(*Shouts.*) Alexei, did we pass Newark?

ALEXEI (*off*). We're near Grant-ham.

ANDRIUS. Grant-ham? Grant-ham.

English place names are crap as well!

Look, Spalding. Spent a month picking daffodils in Spalding. Ever done that?

VICTOR *shakes his head.*

Ten hours picking daffodils and you start to hate daffodils. A week picking daffodils and even the faintest whiff of daffodil makes you heave. A month picking daffodils and you're ready to eliminate all living daffodils from Planet Earth with Agent Orange. But, I have to say, three months of sorting fish guts makes you hanker after those fucking little daffodils again. Okay, Grant-ham, got it, yes.

ALEXEI *enters, hands covered with oil.*

ALEXEI. Steering's fucked. Fuel tank leaks. Spare tyre's balder than Khruschev. We're walking.

ALEXEI *walks off again.*

ANDRIUS. Where's the tour bus, as promised, Alexei? You know, the one with air con, DVDs, coke, stewardesses pleasuring us? Victor and I request a seatbelt at the very least which we are prepared to share. One fucking seatbelt. Victor and I request animal rights in the absence of human rights.

(*Shouts.*) Alexei, Victor and I request the right to be treated as humanely as cows. At the very least. Minimum wage we're prepared to pass over.

ALEXEI (*re-enters on mobile*). You are couple of cows. You're couple of cunts, too. Oh – okay – (*On the phone.*) Mr Grimmer, Alexei again, okay, err, we, we have problem, problem – need speak, need… problem.

Just pick the fucking thing up!

ALEXEI *hurls the phone away in frustration.*

Silence. Cars pass.

VICTOR. Smoke?

Here.

He shows the packet.

ANDRIUS. You sure, peasant?

VICTOR. Sure. Baltic prick.

ALEXEI *laughs*.

Take one.

ANDRIUS. Sure.

VICTOR. Alexei?

ALEXEI. Give me two.

VICTOR. Fine. Take two.

ALEXEI. Okay, I'll take three then.

ANDRIUS. Me too. Red Cross delivery.

They laugh.

VICTOR. Take the packet, man.

ALEXEI. What?

ANDRIUS. It's his saint's day, clearly.

VICTOR. Take the packet.

ALEXEI. Feeling flush?

VICTOR. Take it. It's a packet of cigarettes.

Take it. Shit. Are we in the Gulag?

Take the whole thing. What are we – white cargo?

ALEXEI *does*.

ANDRIUS. Marlboro Lights.

ALEXEI. Flash fuck.

VICTOR. Cigarettes, for God's sake.

Act like peasants, they'll treat us like peasants.

Even the trashiest British guy smokes Marlboro Lights.

ALEXEI *counts the cigarettes.*

ANDRIUS. How d'you afford these?

VICTOR. Worked eighty hours last week. Eighty.

ANDRIUS. Pace yourself, comrade. You'll piss the local proles off. Let alone your fellow serfs.

VICTOR. Napped in the toilets. In a cubicle.

Chewed coffee granules.

ANDRIUS. Were you rewarded for your labours?

VICTOR. I intend to be.

ALEXEI *and* ANDRIUS *laugh.*

ANDRIUS. I wish you the best of luck.

VICTOR. I don't need luck, I've got a contract.

He gets the contract from his pocket.

You didn't get a contract?

ALEXEI. Grimmer keeps all the paperwork.

VICTOR. Well, I demanded a contract. And I know a bit about contracts – drawn up enough of the buggers for my workers.

ANDRIUS. You had workers? What, as in underlings?

VICTOR. Well, I ran a factory. I owned a factory.

ALEXEI. You never owned a fucking factory.

ANDRIUS. Oh, I dunno, Ukraine's a pretty crazy place. Going concern, was it? Balalaikas for the tone-deaf?

VICTOR. We made sausages.

ALEXEI *and* ANDRIUS *laugh.*

Yes. You find that funny. Well, I had a hundred sausage-rollers and sausage-packers and sausage-smokers and I drew up their contracts, so yeah, I know about contracts, and this contract'll tell you what our employers stole from us all last night.

Pause.

ALEXEI. Last night was bad luck.

VICTOR. Wasn't it. Caught you out.

ALEXEI. It caught every fucker out.

VICTOR. You reckon? No surprise to Davies, to Grimmer, to me.

ANDRIUS. Victor, you're so full of secrets today.

Did you have a little liaison last night? Am I smelling something nice under the tang of fish?

ALEXEI. Fucking some Scottish bint.

VICTOR. Maybe.

ANDRIUS. Not the lovely Miss Strang? You sly old Slav.

ALEXEI. Oh, good luck to him. Not fucked a living thing in years.

ANDRIUS. Yeah, we'll pass over the dead things.

ALEXEI. Must like the taste of sausage.

ANDRIUS. Pretty garlicky taste, though, yeah?

The two laugh, slightly wildly.

VICTOR. I didn't make the sausages myself. I paid women to make the sausages. Those sausages were so good you'd weep to smell them. Pink as the flesh in a woman, pinker, softer. My girls touched those sausages with more tenderness than they touched their own kids. You want to talk about sausages? Or do you want to talk about why we're stuck under the wrong sky working for monkeys?

Davies called immigration. Grimmer took his cut. Thirty workers, two factories, one month's wage bill.

ALEXEI. Grimmer knew nothing about it! It was a bad break, it was a random –

VICTOR. Alexei, wake from your dream! Davies cuts his overheads to zero, gets a clean bill of health with the law, Grimmer gets ten grand for one phone call: beats thirty pieces of silver.

ALEXEI. Now you shut up, you cheeky – Shut your cheeky fucking mouth –

VICTOR. We've been robbed! These guys are thieves and they robbed us.

ALEXEI. Mr Grimmer, okay, gave me, yeah, more work, yeah, for more fucking pay, yeah, in one year than I got out of motherfucking Yeltsin or Putin in ten –

VICTOR. Yeah, it's not where we came from, it's where we –

ALEXEI. Okay, okay – last year I was in Grozny, my friend; okay, my CO lent me to farmers to dig ditches for a bottle of fucking vodka, right; my commanding officer, okay – Had to buy my own boots, my fucking boots, my own boots, to go out there, every day, man, every fucking day, go out there to face Muslim bullets – for this what am I paid, what do I receive – nothing, not a kopek, yeah. Grimmer is my father, my mother, my brother; he can suck my cock, he can kick my ass, he can fuck me up the ass, I am in his debt and so are you and you, okay?

He sits and rubs his face in his hands.

VICTOR. It's not where we came from, it's where we are, right?

Pause.

ANDRIUS. Alexei's right. God bless Mr Grimmer. My brother teaches in Vilnius University, teaches Lithuanian history no less. A short course perhaps, but a fine course. He studied ten years to teach this course. For his labours he earns less than I get sorting carrots.

I tell him this regularly to make him angry.

Pause.

VICTOR. You're getting on for thirty, Andrius?

ANDRIUS. I'm old enough.

VICTOR. Alexei's what, forty-odd, I'm getting there. Born in a country formerly known as the Union of Soviet Socialist Republics?

ANDRIUS. Yeah, yeah, born under occupation.

VICTOR. Occupation?

Oh, you did okay out of it. Jobs for life, yes, free healthcare, free education, free housing, no, you didn't complain then.

ANDRIUS. Fuck you. My dad was jailed. For 'Nationalist Deviations'. He flew a fucking flag. So fuck you, Ukrainian.

VICTOR. Now the EU occupies you. Like it any better?

ANDRIUS. We are a free state. I am a citizen of Europe.

VICTOR. You enjoying your freedom?

ANDRIUS. Yes. Well. Not as much as I had hoped.

VICTOR. And Alexei, you're what – Moldovan?

ALEXEI. Russian-Moldovan! On my mother's side.

VICTOR. So, all of us, born in a superpower, all of us, whoever we are now, children of an empire, a vast shit-kicking empire, yeah, which gave Americans nightmares and horsewhipped Hitler and sent heroes and Sputniks and dogs into space!

ALEXEI. Oh God, yeah, those funny little dogs. Laika.

VICTOR. Exactly, Laika, exactly.

ALEXEI. Fucking little Laika, yes. Oh, and there was, what's her name, Belka too.

ANDRIUS. Belka was before my time. Well, actually Laika was before my time too.

ALEXEI. And the other one, what was her name – ?

VICTOR. Strelka.

ALEXEI. Shit, poor little Strelka.

They think about this.

VICTOR. And look at us now, where we are, what we are, here, look at us. Sat in the dirt, worked like niggers and we're grateful.

Silence.

ALEXEI. No, I don't go back to Moldova. What the fuck is
Moldova, it's a slum. My brother, Misha, he dreams of a
better life in Romania. In Romania! No, everybody leaves,
everybody good leaves, well, who could stay?

ANDRIUS. In Kaunas, my town, there's this street, Liberty
Avenue; you know it? Longest street in Europe, truly, lime
trees all along; so cool, when it's sunny on Liberty Avenue,
and the foreign girls come out, English girls, American girls,
no bras or nothing, MP3s, chic little cut-off tops, and you sit
in a square under the lime trees, eat a pastry and – it's… very
– nice. At night, it changes; at night the junkies jack up and
die in the cold and you don't see the moon for the cranes and
the cops haul the drunks into vans and every now and then
some kid jumps off the bridge into one river or another and,
then, then, well, you want to be somewhere else, y'know.

Pause.

What's your alternative suggestion, comrade?

VICTOR. We do this ourselves. Run this ourselves.

For ourselves.

ANDRIUS. Sure, sure, with our mastery of English and our
great working relationship with the authorities.

VICTOR. You speak English.

ANDRIUS. Not good enough for the English.

VICTOR. It's just words. I speak it better every day. Every day
I pick up papers from the bins, read street signs, listen to the
works' radio, read magazines on fish.

ALEXEI. Fuck personnel officers.

ANDRIUS *laughs*.

You're insane.

VICTOR. I am not talking now, not talking yet.

Now we comply, all the better to take the opportunities that
come.

We flatter, we question, we learn.

ALEXEI. They'll cut your throat like a pig.

VICTOR. They'd like you to think that.

ALEXEI. They'll cut your head off, friend.

VICTOR. Alexei, this is not crime. This is not war.

This is business.

ALEXEI's mobile rings; they scramble around for it,
VICTOR gets it.

VICTOR (*on the phone*). Mr Grimmer. Hello. Yes, Victor, yes.
Yes, I hear you. Yes, problem with minibus. Grantham. Yes,
Grantham. Okay. Okay. Okay. Okay. Yes. Thank you, thank
you. Bye-bye, okay.

He wants us to walk to Grantham services. Ten miles south.

ANDRIUS. Ten miles? He's taking the piss.

ALEXEI. What about the van?

VICTOR. He says leave it here. Says that if anyone asks we say
we're students.

ANDRIUS. Can't he even come and pick us up, tight-arse?

ALEXEI starts.

VICTOR. He's the boss, right.

Pause.

ALEXEI. Let's get moving.

(*To* VICTOR.) Or've you got a better idea?

VICTOR. No, no. I like a good walk. Good look at the land.
Fields of daffodils as big as the steppes. Just like home.

They walk.

Scene Four

A squalid room in a remote farmhouse in Norfolk; the next day.
ALEXEI, ANDRIUS, VICTOR *stand by their mattresses;*
GRIMMER *with them.*

GRIMMER. Cold Harbour Farm. Okay, hardly the Hilton.

He laughs.

But, you know, des res in its own way.

Away from it all, off the beaten track.

Extensive views on all sides.

Yeah, it has its plusses, this place.

The three-to-a-room thing's temporary.

Back fire stairs are dodgy.

Don't open that window, this window here.

Don't touch that window. Don't touch these sockets.

ANDRIUS. No curtains.

GRIMMER. What's that?

ANDRIUS. No curtains.

GRIMMER. Oh, you like your curtains, do you?

ANDRIUS. Hard to sleep.

GRIMMER. Get one of the Portuguese girls to run you up
    something. I don't want any music, any noise after nine.
    Yeah? No noise. Old dear who owns the estate's very
    respectable, genteel. Batty.

Old Norfolk girl, old money gone bad. She might look in on
    you, visit you, yeah? She's not entirely up to speed on the,
    err, the multi-occupancy, so should she look in on you,
    should she do that, I want the mattresses out, bags out, I
    want you out. Yeah? Yeah? Give me something back here.

VICTOR. Understood, Mr Grimmer.

GRIMMER. Okay. I mean, there's far worse. I could show you far worse. Seriously.

ALEXEI. We have been in worse.

GRIMMER. Not your usual ebullient self, Alexei.

Homesick are you, mate?

Okay, I'd better push off.

He turns to go.

ANDRIUS. Mr Grimmer. Where is shower?

GRIMMER. He's a quick one, this one. What's that?

ALEXEI. He asks about shower.

GRIMMER. There's what, no shower? There's a standpipe, isn't there? Course there's no shower, there's no water plumbed in. This is country living.

What you worried about – curtains, showers?

VICTOR. We shower in factory.

GRIMMER. Exactly. Exactly.

Lot of complaints. That's disappointing.

I've stuck by you. I got you lot out in time. If it weren't for my swift action you'd be on the first plane to Stalingrad. Right? Alexei?

ALEXEI. Maybe.

GRIMMER. 'Maybe'? I expect something a little more demonstrative than that.

VICTOR. You protect us.

GRIMMER. Yes I do. 'Cos actually I believe in the right to work. Look, I better get on, I've got this guy in Soham sitting on my dick –

ANDRIUS. May we have wages now? Unpaid wages.

VICTOR. Andrius!

GRIMMER. What did you say?

ANDRIUS. Month of work for SeaFresh.

Pause.

GRIMMER. Okay, Davies, I'll be honest with you, Phil Davies is a total fucking shark, I realise that now. Some of the people in this business, they are cynical.

VICTOR. Yes.

ALEXEI. Lost money.

GRIMMER. Alexei, are you going to get your head out my arse any time soon? Perhaps you'd care to explain that I am not empowered to cough up cash I don't happen to have.

ANDRIUS. How do we live?

GRIMMER. You know what, you're impertinent.

VICTOR. Please, Mr Grimmer, my friends and I have no – money.

GRIMMER. Well, you should look after your money.

Not my fault, right – am I right – if you have no money.

VICTOR. But ask Davies for money –

GRIMMER. I'll talk to him –

ALEXEI. Talk!

GRIMMER. Look, as you are so – rightly – pissed off about this, I will, look – hang on –

He reaches into his pocket.

I look after my people, I am noted for that.

Here, what you owed, Andrius?

ANDRIUS. Five hundred.

GRIMMER. Oh, behave – I'm not Roman Abramovich!

ANDRIUS. Month's money.

GRIMMER. Look, I've got a hundred here, no deductions, a bonus, won't even pass through the books. Goodwill.

Pause.

Make it hundred-fifty.

VICTOR. Thank you.

GRIMMER. Nice to hear that word. You rarely do in this show. Step up then.

He counts out to them.

Now let's stop scratching our bumholes and start the graft, yeah.

VICTOR. I have question. About wages.

Deductions? Just question. I ask our rate.

GRIMMER. Who? Who did you ask?

VICTOR. Personnel –

The others smile.

GRIMMER. You don't do that, okay.

VICTOR. Rate was good.

GRIMMER. Yeah. And your point is?

VICTOR. After deductions.

GRIMMER. Rent. Transport.

VICTOR. Good, good. But please explain – VAT?

GRIMMER. I do it by the book.

VICTOR. Yes. But – income tax?

GRIMMER. I do it by the book.

You're taking issue with me now.

With my employment practices, yeah?

You want to claim that back? From Inland Revenue? I'll get you the forms. Try your luck.

VICTOR. I am curious. In Ukraine I ran factory.

GRIMMER. Yeah, well, it's still there, right. The Ukraine.

Last time I looked.

VICTOR. But: equipment? What is this?

GRIMMER. The factory pass on their costs to me.

As far as the factory and the fucking personnel and that crowd, you lot do not exist, cannot exist. You do not use consumables. You do not eat in canteens. You do not dump in the staff bogs. You don't like your wages, go and throw yourself on the Immigration people. Try living on a tenner a week. Try living on a phonecard and a packet of fags.

VICTOR. Thank you again, Mr Grimmer.

GRIMMER. What?

VICTOR. You answer questions. Thank you.

GRIMMER. I wouldn't take the piss out of me, son.

ANDRIUS. He means it.

VICTOR *tries to shake* GRIMMER's *hand*.

VICTOR. Mr Grimmer, you do excellent good job.

Truly. I thank you. Andrius thanks you.

Andrius.

ANDRIUS *walks over and shakes his hand*.

Thank him, Andrius.

ANDRIUS. I am most grateful, Mr Grimmer.

GRIMMER. Well –

VICTOR. Alexei.

ALEXEI *walks over, the same*.

ALEXEI. You are friend to Russians.

GRIMMER. Well, I… I should think so…

VICTOR. Victor.

GRIMMER. Victor. Yeah. I look out for my people. Yeah.

You ever see that film, that film, what was it, that black-and-white film? About the Jews and that guy, that big Irish fella played him, that guy who bought the Jews, sort of saved them from the Nazis. Useless on names. Big Irish guy.

Set somewhere Polish, was it?

I suppose I'm a bit like him. The big Irish fella?

Bringing you lot... doing it fair and that. Yeah?

VICTOR. We have much, much to thank you for, to respect you for.

GRIMMER. Well, don't overdo it. Okay. Nice one. Goodnight then. And no noise, alright. No shouting. No –

VICTOR. No music.

GRIMMER. Yeah.

He goes.

VICTOR. One day we will fuck your wife.

ANDRIUS. We will fuck your daughters.

ALEXEI. We will fuck you.

VICTOR *gets a tape-recorder out and places a cassette in. He plays Led Zeppelin's 'Immigrant Song'. It plays out the scene.*

Blackout.

End of Act One.

ACT TWO

Scene One

GRIMMER*'s garden in a house outside Ely; early autumn. The bells are ringing on the hour.* VICTOR, ANDRIUS *and* ALEXEI *are digging, stripped to the waist or in vests.*

ANDRIUS. This is killing my back.

ALEXEI. You've got no technique.

VICTOR. Andrius is strictly white-collar.

ALEXEI. Dough for hands, shit for brains.

ANDRIUS. Give me a motherboard and I'll show you technique.

VICTOR. Watch, Alexei; light with the shaft, bend at the knees, good rhythm going, blade goes in, foot on the lip, depress the foot, drive it down, and tip up and off with the earth.

ANDRIUS. Why are we breaking our backs for charity?

VICTOR. It's all goodwill.

ALEXEI. Everything's goodwill with that cunt.

VICTOR. He brought us here for a reason.

Do the Poles get to dig his garden?

ANDRIUS. We're obviously more of a soft touch.

VICTOR. He's coming. Smile.

GRIMMER *comes out to them. They smile.*

GRIMMER. That soil's a clayey old bugger, ain't it. Right, dockey time. Pot of tea warming in the kitchen, Alexei.

Oh, Andrius, keep a weather eye out for the fella with the mulch. I asked for woodchip not dung, don't let him drop off any dung, he'll try that. Round the front, there. Good lad.

ANDRIUS *goes off,* ALEXEI *too.*

Ah, look at that. The foreign element: (*He weeds.*)
bindweed's a virulent bastard.

You got to be so vigilant, yeah. See them hostas here, lovely
little plant, resilient, low-maintenance, turn your back on
'em, you get petals with more holes than a ruddy cheese-
grater; bloody snails!

Where's the thrushes when you need them?

You a gardener yourself, Victor?

VICTOR. No. No gardens in Ukraine.

GRIMMER. You're kidding me?

VICTOR. Allotment. Not garden.

Communists not like gardens. Gardening: bourgeois!

GRIMMER. Well, that's why we like it. In England.

Bet you don't get views as good as that though – twenty mile
in all directions – Chatteris, Downham Market, Wisbech;
black earth. My domain, that.

VICTOR. Like Ukraine. Flat. Sky. Flat.

GRIMMER. Yeah, no frills round here.

Pause. They look.

It's a queer old world, Victor, when a fella like yourself,
management material, ends up digging my garden for
tuppence.

'Cos you had a factory, right?

VICTOR. Yes. Buy '92. Before: state factory.

Food bad. Nobody work, nobody clean. State, err – private?

GRIMMER. Privatise?

VICTOR. Exact, privatise, '92. I buy.

GRIMMER. Where d'you get that sort of money then?

VICTOR. Save money.

GRIMMER. No, your lot didn't have that sort of money.

VICTOR. Sure, save money.

GRIMMER. Don't pull my dick and I won't pull yours, Victor.

Where's it all gone, your factory?

VICTOR. Burn. Last year. Enemy burn. Land more, err, value.
Enemy want me go, but no, good place – road to Kiev,
Kharkiv, Odessa; export start, Germany. Enemy – threat.
'No, I businessman.' Enemy say, 'Pay me'; 'No,' I say, 'no,
this my – domain – I – '

Makes gesture.

GRIMMER. Grow?

VICTOR. Exact – grow, yes! Tell police, police: 'No make
trouble.' Tell mayor, mayor enemy friend, fire start, tell fire
station, nobody come, try stop fire, no-fucking-good. Sorry –
for bad word, sorry. My country: *vorovskoy mir*.

GRIMMER. What's that?

VICTOR. *Vorovskoy mir*. 'Thief world.' World of thief. Not
accept. Come here. World of law, business. World of garden.

Pause.

GRIMMER. Shocking story. Awful, some of your stories.

Everyone of you's got one.

Okay, refreshments. Alexei, good chap.

ALEXEI *comes out of the house with a tray of tea.*

How do you take it, lads? Milk first or last?

VICTOR. No milk. Please.

ALEXEI. Me neither.

GRIMMER. No milk, very posh. Sugar. Help yourself, each to
your own.

VICTOR *puts in five sugars.*

Yes, it's a queer old world. Like us, chatting away, like it's the most normal thing. Incredible. You know, when I started this agency I didn't have a single foreign name on the books. All locals, Cambridgeshire people, Norfolk people. Nice in a way. But you know what, and I hate saying this, I feel awful saying this, they were no good – When push came to shove, when things started really taking off in this sector, the Big Four, the supermarkets started to push the costs and the farmers and the processors were coming to me and saying, 'Mike, Mike, we need people, we need all the people you can get.' – Seriously, I'd have farmers in tears 'cos they couldn't meet some spec for a procurer in Asda; and I couldn't help them, I said sorry, half the girls went sick or were up the duff or were putting in claims for RSI, I mean, excuse the French, but what the fuck is RSI?

Now you got chaps like yourselves – ten-hour shifts – no problem –

VICTOR. I like to work.

ALEXEI. All of us – like to work.

GRIMMER. You do, you do. Call you up all hours, no special pleading. Tea alright, there?

VICTOR. Delicious.

GRIMMER. Yeah, good stuff. But I need the people.

And here's the thing, Alexei, you don't get me the numbers these days, you know what I mean?

ALEXEI. My contacts, err, say more difficult to get –

GRIMMER. No, mate, sorry, I have this thing about excuses.

Just don't hear them. You do not get the numbers.

Maybe Victor here might do better, I dunno.

VICTOR. Mr Grimmer. I bring you villages. I bring you cities.

I bring you Ukraine.

Pause.

GRIMMER. Heard that alright.

I need a guaranteed supply.

And, this is the thing, I can't be seen to be involved – in supply.

VICTOR. No problem. Keep me – (*He makes a gesture with his arm.*) away. You want labour, you don't want keep it. Okay.

GRIMMER. Sure. Arm's length.

VICTOR. 'Arm's length', yes, good.

GRIMMER. Well, that's what you end up doing more and more during these politically correct times – sub-contracting. Your British person, they want the world on a plate and they want Bob Geldof too – they want their last-minute iceberg lettuce in March, but you tell them how it got there so crunchy and cheap, they get all squeamish.

VICTOR. They not need know – how. Keep me – arm's length!

(*He whistles.*) No see, know, no worry.

GRIMMER. Yeah, sub-contract – all down the line. Supermarkets to packager, packager to farmer, farmer to me, and me – to you.

VICTOR. Labour – here, there, gone.

He rubs his hands as if cleaning them. ANDRIUS enters with a very heavy mulch sack.

GRIMMER. What is it, lad? Woodchip or dung?

ANDRIUS. Don't know.

GRIMMER. Stick your hand in.

ANDRIUS. I don't – Okay.

GRIMMER. Right in. Now, does it smell like shit?

ANDRIUS. Yes.

GRIMMER. Take it back, I want woodchip.

ANDRIUS starts to drag the sack off again.

Useless fuckers, that lot. Still, get trade rates.

He looks at VICTOR; VICTOR *smiles; suddenly they laugh.*

Okay, let's give it a whirl, trial period. Few months, review it
– okay. Set up your own firm, your own outfit, with my...
protection. See where we are by Christmas.

VICTOR. Okay.

GRIMMER. 'Okay'!

They shake hands.

What we gonna call you? 'Slavs R Us'?

VICTOR. Sorry?

GRIMMER. Little joke.

VICTOR. No, have good name.

GRIMMER. You been thinking a lot about this?

VICTOR. Of course. Study you.

GRIMMER. Could do a lot worse. What's your name then?

VICTOR. Fast Labour!

GRIMMER. 'Fast Labour'! (*He laughs.*) That's... no, that's –
hardly... subtle, is it?

VICTOR. Fast to work, fast to come, fast to go. Fast Labour.

GRIMMER. Alright. Fast Labour. Okay, you keep your own
books, own address, your own people. And you just invoice
me, y'know, as and when. I'll front up accommodation,
transport, but you provide. You deal with... paperwork. You
got a mobile?

VICTOR. No.

GRIMMER (*to* ALEXEI). Got your mobile, mate?

ALEXEI *gets his out.*

That's a nice piece. I give you that?

ALEXEI. Sure.

GRIMMER. Those fucking Finns, eh.

You know what, I don't reckon you'll be needing that now.

ALEXEI. I need my gear.

GRIMMER. Can I be frank with you, mate? You're a bit stolid. A bit lacking in imagination, bit volatile, right. Give us the phone.

Pause.

VICTOR (*in Russian*). This is just for now.

ALEXEI (*in Russian*). Oh yeah.

VICTOR (*in Russian*). Submit to this cunt now and tomorrow I will make you a prince.

GRIMMER. Less of the jabber! Hand it over.

ALEXEI *spits on the phone.*

Oh, get out of my garden, you *child.*

ALEXEI. Sure, for sure.

ALEXEI *walks off.* GRIMMER *wipes the spit off with a handkerchief.*

GRIMMER. Touchy bugger. I'll cover calls, for now.

I mean, within reason. Course you're not… legit. Are you? You don't have to be coy, Victor, we're grown-ups here.

VICTOR. Not. Legit.

GRIMMER. Be easier having you overground.

Could make a good case for asylum. Political oppression. Extortion. Mafia. If you don't have a case, who has? Yeah, my brother-in-law's in Immigration.

Job's hardly serious. What, twenty officers, five hundred square miles? Hardly serious.

If this endeavour works out, I might go and have a little chat with my brother-in-law – pick his brains.

No promises.

And what about that Scottish lass, HR, lovely little tits?

VICTOR. Anita?

GRIMMER. Anita, yeah. Could come in handy. On the phone and that. They don't like to hear an accent, people round here. It's like these call centres; I mean, I'm the worst, I can tell a Sanjay from a Sandra in seconds – and they do try hard, those Indians. But foreign shows, don't it?

ANDRIUS comes back with another sack of mulch.

ANDRIUS. He say you order, err – fish, blood and bone.

GRIMMER. I don't want anything smelly. Woodchip, mate, woodchip.

ANDRIUS. Woodchip, okay.

He drags it off again.

GRIMMER. Right, Victor, little thing I always say, formality really: don't take liberties. Understand? What's given can be taken away.

Pause. VICTOR realises the meeting's over, starts to go.

Nice thing about autumn's the leaf-drop.

Uninterrupted view of the cathedral.

Patio-heater, hot toddy, cigar.

This country can be a paradise, Victor, if you know how to behave.

Scene Two

A service station on the A1 near Grantham; a week later.
ANITA *and* VICTOR *are drinking coffee.*

VICTOR. I like this place.

ANITA. It's cheap. I hate it.

VICTOR. No, I like. Whole world come here. Family.

Truckers. Look, that guy, Albanian pimp, yes.

Yes, look, pimp, by family.

ANITA. He's just a lorry driver or something.

VICTOR. No, no. Look, pimp go with man from family in
toilet, look.

Wait. Now girl. Where she from?

ANITA. God knows – Sweden, mebbe.

VICTOR. Sweden, no, no Swedish whores! Latvian.

Okay, there she go.

ANITA. She's the girl who served me coffee!

Turning a trick in her fag-break?

You make the world nastier than it is.

VICTOR. No, no. Everyone busy, busy. I like this place.
Smoke?

He lights up.

ANITA. It's non-smoking, here. It's the law.

VICTOR. It's a café.

ANITA. The floor manager's staring at you – Victor, put it –

She snatches it from his mouth, holds it.

VICTOR. Nobody care.

ANITA. Put it out.

VICTOR. Okay, okay. No ashtray.

ANITA. Evidently!

VICTOR stands and extinguishes the cigarette on the floor with his foot.

Got yourself some decent shoes, then.

VICTOR. You like these shoes?

He takes one off.

ANITA. Don't take it off in here. There's food about.

God almighty, look at you.

VICTOR. Reebok. In Ukraine, three-month wage.

Generic. Look at this. Cushion. Beautiful. Truly.

He kisses it.

ANITA. You crazed loon, you.

She laughs despite herself.

VICTOR. Buy four pairs. Send three home. For girls.

ANITA. Girls? You've got daughters?

VICTOR. No, no, of course. Nieces.

ANITA. Man a mystery, you.

VICTOR. You think I lie?

ANITA. Oh, I don't know what to think about you.

VICTOR. Well, believe in me. In what I believe.

He goes to kiss her; she pushes him away. Pause.

ANITA. Let me tell you a few things about British women, Victor. Firstly, if they give you their bed and their body they expect in the very least a goodbye kiss or a note on the mirror or some shred of evidence that they're not a tart; and secondly, they'll not be won over with a caffé latte and a quick snog in a Moto.

Pause.

VICTOR. Okay. This is business, okay, Anita, business now.

ANITA. Oh, now you're Alan fucking Sugar.

VICTOR. You management material, Anita.

ANITA. 'Management material'? You been reading the *Financial Times*?

VICTOR. Serious, serious. Drive German car. Live in detached house. Have big garden. Really.

ANITA. My flat's okay, my car's French and I hate gardening.

VICTOR. Live like Ukrainian. Why?

ANITA. It's the way I am and you keep out.

VICTOR. I learn something in this country.

There is no good reason to be poor.

ANITA. Och, I'm not poor, I'm good.

VICTOR. Anita, what stops you from being rich lady?

This stops you, this, your mind.

ANITA. I'm not some shark, okay.

VICTOR. Why not? Why not be shark? You prefer, what you prefer to be – what fish sharks eat?

ANITA. I don't know, plankton, it's irrelevant, shut up.

VICTOR. You prefer be sharkfood? Be shark.

Sharks are brave. Sharks are cool.

ANITA. Sharks are nasty bastards who fuck over their pals.

VICTOR. Maybe. Maybe. But to other sharks they are lovely.

To shark children they are daddy shark.

Shark wives love them just the same.

In Ukraine I think I shark.

No, I was not shark. I was sharkfood. I was plankton.

ANITA. This is getting stupid, this shark thing.

VICTOR. Become a shark, Anita.

He tries to kiss her; she pushes him away.

ANITA. I liked you better when you spoke less. Who taught you all this… language?

VICTOR. Watch television, listen radio. Talking radio. All time. Very good radio. Wogan I not like.

Television: *Countdown* good.

For words. *Weakest Link* very good.

Changing Rooms – brilliant! We need Ukrainian *Changing Rooms*. Err, Baboushka's flat: 'Old lady, out brown carpet, out Brezhnev photo, out net curtain, out candle, out icon. Now look; ah, see: plasma TV screen, whole wall; boom! Da-do rail! Bathroom: power shower.' Heart attack Baboushka. Dead Baboushka.

She laughs, he holds her hand; she breaks away.

ANITA. No, what, what's this about? Work or… love, or what?

VICTOR. Why one or other? Work and love.

Love and work. You think they not one thing. Work here, life there. No – life is work.

Life is work, family, love: all one. You forget basic truth. Love me. Work for me.

ANITA. One at a time.

VICTOR. All at once.

ANITA. Anyway, what's this 'work for you'? Work for what?

VICTOR. Fast Labour.

ANITA. Fast Labour?

VICTOR. Yes. New recruitment agency. Here.

He hands her a typed letter. She reads.

ANITA. This is full of typos.

VICTOR. Good, good, Anita, this is where we need your knowledge. Good, intelligent, checking it out. Good.

He gets out pen.

Please, correct, please.

ANITA. 'Low costs legitimate labour.' From where?

VICTOR. Former Soviet Union.

ANITA. Legitimate?

VICTOR. Of course.

ANITA. Like you?

VICTOR. I have papers – soon.

ANITA. You're a bloody chancer. Economic migrants, right?

VICTOR. People who want to work.

ANITA. Yeah, well, they can do that in your 'former Soviet Union'. I'm sorry. Not interested, not my scene.

She gets up, VICTOR *stays her.*

VICTOR. Sit down, Anita, sit down.

ANITA. Oh, you've got the wrong girl –

VICTOR. I need you, Anita.

ANITA. Look, I really don't have criminal potential, Victor, you know what I'm saying. Yeah, you need someone with a bit of, you know, experience in the 'black economy', bit of a CV, like; best I can offer is smoking a joint, going forty in a thirty zone, and a few dodgy downloads. Try your wee Latvian lassie in the lavs, there.

VICTOR. This humanitarian work.

ANITA. Oh God, that's another cracking little word.

VICTOR. Serious, I am serious, you help people, you help me –

ANITA. I see now that was my biggest mistake.

VICTOR. Sit down, down, no –

He takes her bag from her, knocking the coffee from the table.

ANITA. Stop making a scene. People are staring.

VICTOR. Yeah, I make a scene, for sure, big scene.

ANITA. Victor! Keep your voice down.

VICTOR. Listen to me.

ANITA. Okay, okay.

She sits.

VICTOR. I come from ugly town in Ukraine.

Think worst British town. My town is worse.

Think jobs, no money for jobs. Police: not paid.

Teacher not paid, teaching.

ANITA. So life's pretty tough in the Ukraine, Victor.

It's not actually my fault.

VICTOR. No, no, listen, until I here I no idea how bad.

No idea. Shittiest place in your country is paradise. Nothing in town, nothing. Once, college, agriculture. Closed.

Truck factory. Closed. Tram stopped.

Weeds grow in street. My family:

VICTOR acts this next section out on the table using sugar and salt and pepper and sauce.

Every day, Mother go to bus station; headscarf, jumpers, coat – cloth – lay down; here, sunflower seeds; old boot she find, cleaned; egg from, err, err, chicken; my father – take car apart – spark plug, okay, hubcap, spanner; who buy? Okay – who buy egg? Okay? Just to buy, what, to buy bread – my aunt – brother –

ANITA. You know, I am sincerely – sorry – for your, y'know, family but, but, I fail to see how your country's problems're gonna be fixed by turning my country into some sort of free-for-all. Fine, fine, let in the poor souls who're in trouble, your Iraqis, your wee African kiddies, whomsoever, for sure, for sure, but I honestly fail to see why we, here, have to be some sort of job centre for half the fucking planet.

VICTOR. Where we go? Poland? Poland worse.

Austria? Old people and mountains and police.

Germany? France? Turks, Arabs. Your country, 'Hello, come in, are you skilled, okay, are you fit, okay, welcome.' Welcome. Treat you like a dog but welcome. Since I come to country, cost not one penny. Make money in this country, for this country. Whose job I take? I make jobs, look, look at me. Pay tax, okay, I pay tax. Mr Brown, were he meet me, Mr Gordon Brown thank me. Not say this, cannot say this, British people afraid of this, but I see Gordon Brown's face and know in heart he welcome me.

ANITA. Oh God, dream on, Victor.

VICTOR. Do – not – laugh at me, Anita.

Pause.

ANITA. You're so… fragile.

VICTOR *gets up.*

VICTOR. What you pay for gas? Here, okay. Fifty?

ANITA. Oh, shut up.

VICTOR. No, I go I – I pay, err, expenses, how much how much – for coffee, ten? Pizza, bed for night, another thirty: okay?

He's leaving.

ANITA. Wait. Stop.

Okay, this is shameful, but you know what, you know what I did, Victor, you know what I did here – I booked a double room. Okay. In the fucking Travelodge. A chalet. So, err, would you like to pay for that? 'Cos I just thought we could go there and we could hold each other and, and –

She bursts into tears.

Oh – now look at me – I – I am fundamentally a simple person, I never before knew about any of this, seriously.

But you came to me and you loved me and you opened up a door in my life and you went and slammed it shut in my face. Do you have any notion what you made me feel?

VICTOR. I never ever understand you, Anita.

He laughs.

ANITA. Well, you're a stupid – shite and I'm a – bloody – fool.

He takes her and she holds him. Silence. She breaks free.

Listen, I need to, I need a walk. I can't think about this… with you – looking – at me. I need to know what I think on my own. I need to just –

She puts a key on the table.

Chalet five. Booked under me, under Strang.

If you're there when I get back and still there in the morning then… then we can talk about… this.

Yeah, I need a walk.

She goes.

VICTOR. Beautiful, beautiful shark.

He goes.

Scene Three

The living room of a rented terraced house in King's Lynn; winter, approaching Christmas. A table, not enough chairs; laptop, papers. Plastic Christmas tree. Morning: ANDRIUS, ALEXEI eating bowls of borscht; on the wall, maps of Eurasia crudely drawn, of Britain, of East Anglia.

ALEXEI. Kilo of beetroot. Two onions. Fresh dill.

ANDRIUS. Dill, okay.

ALEXEI. A shake of vodka. Cubes of pork, chopped, diced. Sour cream.

ANDRIUS. Well, it's good.

ALEXEI. Grandmother's recipe.

ANDRIUS. Thank you, Moldovan grandmother.

ALEXEI. She was a witch who beat my mother.

They eat.

ANDRIUS. That's very good, yes. (*Yawns.*) Couldn't get off last night.

ALEXEI. Me neither.

ANDRIUS. Heard you snoring.

ALEXEI. Heard you wanking.

ANDRIUS. Oh. Okay. Extreme provocation.

ALEXEI. They were next to my wall.

He makes some obscene gesture.

Him grunting like a borzoi on heat –

ANDRIUS. Her screaming like an elk.

ALEXEI. You've heard an elk fucking?

ANDRIUS. She sounds the way it would sound.

ANDRIUS's mobile goes.

(*On the phone.*) Yes, hello, Mr Woodford, yes, Fast Labour, correct, how are you this morning?

Your turkeys are happy turkeys, I hope.

How do we help you?

ANITA enters, putting on lipstick.

ALEXEI. I make coffee.

ANITA. Grand. 'How can we help you?'

ANDRIUS. More is fine, more is very fine. Is that to – to where – Fay-ken-ham –

ANITA (*to* ANDRIUS). Here, here, north Norfolk.

She draws a mark.

ANDRIUS. Okay, okay, we bring twenty tough Latvian ladies, very dexterous girls, very good 'motor co-ordination', you breaking up on me –

Alexei, fifteen, night shift, this place –

ALEXEI. Cool.

ANDRIUS. Yes, you back again very clear, very nice.

Okay, fifteen ready for work 6 p.m. – is there something else we do for you today? Okay, take care now, jolly Christmas.

ANITA. 'Merry', it's 'merry'.

Yeah, good, good but don't fawn on the guy, he'll think you're coming on to him.

ANDRIUS. That is problem?

ANITA. I'm making toast. Anyone want toast?

ALEXEI. Have borscht. On cooker.

ANDRIUS. It's very good, actually.

ANITA. For breakfast? Thought porridge was bad enough.

ALEXEI. Eat borscht all day. Morning, lunch, night. Hot, cold.

Borscht.

ANITA. I'll stick to toast. Where's Victor? Oh, hang on –

Her mobile goes. She drifts off to the kitchen.

Yes, Anita Strang, Fast Labour –

Oh, hello there, yes, you have the property by the – down by the Wash; okay – uh-huh – and how many rooms we talking? Five? And what are you –

ANDRIUS. How much does she know?

ALEXEI. What do you care? She gets us clients.

ANDRIUS. She's up to speed with the Grimmer scam?

ALEXEI. She liaises with him.

ANDRIUS. Yeah, but what about your end of the operation?

ALEXEI. She's got eyes and ears and a brain.

ANDRIUS. Why move her in though? She should be kept at arm's length.

ALEXEI. She's Victor's woman, it's natural.

ANDRIUS. Victor, Victor thinks with his dick –

ALEXEI. Victor's the boss. Your boss, my boss. Okay?

ANDRIUS. He's a dangerous optimist, that's his problem, he actually trusts people.

ALEXEI. Whatever he is, he's put a roof over our heads and food in our bellies and we put up or shut up.

ALEXEI's mobile goes.

Misha, my brother – (*On the phone.*) Where are you? Chisinau good.

Good – You spoke to Svetlana? Yeah, cool.

Three trucks, yes; via Athens-Piraeus –

He checks the map, finding a line down from Moldova to Greece.

No, you take that upfront; I faxed the pro forma through; make good copies, get a thousand upfront.

Western Union, get euros, send it to us at the given address; sure, sure you take your cut.

ANITA's come back in, eating toast, watching ALEXEI.

Excuse me – Anita, twenty students come Friday; 3 a.m.

ANITA. Should have the new flat up and running by then.

I mean, if not, we could double up in – Hang on –

She checks a notebook. VICTOR *enters with a bag of goods.*

VICTOR. Okay, good, good everyone, in here, now. Phones off. Please, finish call, okay. Alexei, four glasses.

Now one drink, no more, Alexei; he'll be here soon – afterwards, then we drink this, and this, and this, and get pissed as fuck.

Unpacks bottles.

Glasses, glasses, good, ten grammes.

ANITA. Shouldn't we hold off till after Grimmer –

VICTOR. We need warming. Business is pleasure.

ALEXEI. Fuck – Lviv vodka.

VICTOR. Lviv vodka. No shit, no headaches – drink of Politburo. The first – Anita, Andrius, Alexei – toast – one, two, three –

ANITA. Err, to friendship –

ANDRIUS. To success!

ALEXEI. To loyalty!

They drink.

VICTOR. Okay, I promise minutes, Andrius, minutes.

ANDRIUS. I'm not fast enough –

ANITA. I'll take them, I can speak and –

VICTOR. Anita, English minutes for Grimmer; Andrius, Russian minutes – okay, first item, I love you all, you know that, a kiss for you all, there, both cheek, yes, okay, and I thank you all for turnover last month of – unbelievable: £100,000. Okay, before wage, before cost, okay, but ten processer, five dairy, six farm; err, total of three hundred people with work, accommodation, transport – major achievement.

ALEXEI. £100,000!

ANDRIUS. Turnover not profit –

ANITA. Halve that –for – ?

VICTOR. Half to Grimmer, but, hard work, head work, fast work – fuck!!! Three month and we go up each month, this is fucking graph up up up! Two, okay, reports, Anita, report, please.

ANITA. Oh, right. It's been, yeah, a productive week; I focused
on Norfolk leads and I was surprised at the demand; I mean,
we've got big family concern, arable farm, packaging, Attle-
borough area here; big beet time for them at the moment and
a canning plant Thetford way, here, we're talking, what,
thirty-minute drive; they're cash largely, they do invoice but,
you know, it's overnight demand and they seem very happy
with the guys we sent over –

ALEXEI (*in Russian*). Moldovans.

VICTOR (*in Russian*). Belarussians. Andrius, you heard from
Minsk?

ANDRIUS (*in Russian*). Minsk's cool.

ANITA. Can we keep this in English?

VICTOR. Sure – logistical – sure –

ANITA. Okay, Lincolnshire's looking tasty, lot of interest around
Boston but, and it's a 'but' I need help on, lots of overlap with
Grimmer there, but you said you'd check that out, Victor –

VICTOR. Not a problem –

ANDRIUS. Well, yeah it's a problem – now –

ANITA. Yeah, I would have thought –

ANDRIUS. We poach, he comes at us –

ALEXEI. 'Poach'?

VICTOR. He need not know it's us –

ANITA. How can he not know?

VICTOR. Simple. Speak to packager, say, here Grimmer's
people; okay, but also here our people, our people better
people, so Grimmer's people, 'Fuck off', say to Grimmer,
'Oh, packaging guy motherfucker, sorry, take maybe one or
two'; but from us he take, ten, maybe twenty from us.

ANITA. He'll check you out.

VICTOR. He's busy, busy: Scotland, Yorkshire, he delegate –
Enough, Andrius next, Anita you –

ANITA. No, well, you'll laugh at this but Davies, you know, Davies, SeaFresh, well, our friend has been leaving messages and I've not got back 'cos I presume that'd be a firm fuck-off 'no' –

VICTOR. No. Get back to him –

ALEXEI. Victor, the guy's evil.

VICTOR. He call us, okay. Why? We have reputation. Get back to him.

ANDRIUS. Stay local.

VICTOR. I want Scotland. I want all Britain.

ANITA. Look, it's not right, it's too soon, Victor –

VICTOR. Think seasons, okay, here spring, summer, there winter; get back to him – Alexei, be quiet.

ANITA. No, I'm not prepared to do that. I know what's on his hard drive.

Pause.

VICTOR. Okay. Good advice. We don't need him. Okay. Andrius –

ANITA. Oh, sorry, one last – Just, we're pretty squeezed on properties, mebbe a caravan park in Chatteris, here – holiday chalets, here. But even working on, what, two to a room –

VICTOR. Four.

ANITA. Four? To a room.

ANDRIUS. Hotbed it. Shifts.

ANITA. What about privacy?

ALEXEI *laughs*.

VICTOR. Not Russian word.

ANITA. Yeah but – even then, if these fifteen are coming – the sanitation, fire risk –

ALEXEI. Use Cold Harbour Farm.

ANDRIUS. That shithole?

ANITA. You are joking –

ALEXEI. We sleep there, two month, Grimmer not use –

ANITA. No, Victor, you said yourself there's cables exposed on the walls, broken windows, no plumbing –

ALEXEI. Four walls and roof. Fine.

ANITA. I think we need to draw a line, right. That's our brand, right. With your people.

Pause.

VICTOR. Keep in reserve. For bottlenecks. Reserve.

ANITA. Minute that. I'll minute that.

VICTOR. Okay, Andrius – language school –

ANDRIUS (*in Russian*). Is this for her to hear?

VICTOR (*in Russian*). Keep it general.

ANITA. What did you say?

ANDRIUS. Yes; excellent language school, best in East Anglia; three teachers; respected Russian linguist, Alexei here, lecturer in comparative languages, our good lady Anita here, and myself, highly respected blah blah blah; borrowed brother's doctorate. Basically, take as many as we want, they get credit from well, any college back home, study for thirty-hour week – get here, study is pretty relaxed and hey, lots and lots of 'work experience'. Lots! I have waiting list.

ANITA. I don't want my name on, on that.

ANDRIUS. Please, lovely 'Nita, I need British name.

ANITA. I'm sorry, there's such a thing as trade description –

ANDRIUS. Miss Honesty, it's just paperwork –

ANITA. That's not the point –

ANDRIUS. Is peanuts compared with –

VICTOR. Andrius!

Pause.

ANITA. Compared with what?

Pause.

VICTOR. Anita, please make cup of thick black coffee, five sugars. I like coffee brew slowly happy, happy to wait.

ANITA. Don't patronise me, Victor.

ALEXEI. Help yourself to borscht, Anita.

ANDRIUS. It's good borscht, truly.

Pause.

ANITA. You lot are weirding me out – Stop staring, okay.

VICTOR. Coffee, five sugars.

ANITA. You keep the minutes. In English.

She goes.

ANDRIUS. Yeah, Alexei and I were wondering the extent to which your – well, what do I call her, your lover – to what extent she is informed about the true nature of our enterprise.

VICTOR. Alexei?

ALEXEI. I said nothing, he's lying.

ANDRIUS. You had natural anxieties.

ALEXEI. I said nothing, you liar.

VICTOR. It's fine, it's okay. Good question. She's… briefed.

ANDRIUS. Fully?

ALEXEI. He answered your question.

VICTOR. She knows what she needs to know.

ANDRIUS. So you're saying, effectively, she's in the dark.

VICTOR. You know I don't lie. I never lie. Alexei, do I lie?

ALEXEI. Never.

ANDRIUS. So for instance, and I know this is none of my business – but she is aware of the existence of your wife? Your daughters?

ALEXEI. That's not relevant. That's out of order.

VICTOR. It's okay, Alexei. She's never asked me, I don't think.

ANDRIUS. Really? You know I doubt that.

VICTOR. Andrius, you know nothing about British women; they're not as hidebound as the girls back home, okay, they look outward, and Anita is a humanitarian –

ANDRIUS *laughs*.

I'm feeling festive today and a little drunk and warm in my belly so I won't take offence at your attitude, Andrius.

ANDRIUS. What is she for? I mean, I'm sure she's a good fuck and that's fine, but if she's more than that –

ALEXEI. That's enough.

VICTOR. She's very good at her job.

ANDRIUS. Love and money don't mix, first rule of business.

ALEXEI. You made your fucking point.

VICTOR. Listen, we're scary, Andrius. Even with a suit and tie, even with a German car and an English accent they are scared of us; Anita relaxes the clients.

ANDRIUS. But does she know where the merchandise comes from, Victor? She any idea how fifty Ukrainian students end up on a ship of the line bound for Felixstowe?

VICTOR. She knows. Everyone in this country knows. They know what they need to know and what they don't want to know, they don't know. And she's made a decision. And for her I play it her way – contract, tax deductions, bank account, minuted meetings –

ANDRIUS. Oh, so you minuted last night?

ALEXEI *slaps* ANDRIUS *around the face*.

ALEXEI. Cheeky fucking child.

VICTOR. Alexei, don't take it upon yourself to protect my honour.

Pause.

ANDRIUS. Got a nosebleed now. Shit.

VICTOR. Get up. You're fine.

ANDRIUS. I'm not fine, in fact –

VICTOR. Get up. Here, a handkerchief. Here.

ANDRIUS. Is he going to apologise for, for – this?

VICTOR. Alexei.

ALEXEI. He doesn't respect –

VICTOR. Alexei.

ALEXEI. I apologise.

ANDRIUS. Good, good, don't – I don't give a shit what you do in the sack, Victor – your sexual prowess is, you know, apparent – but when she finds out, when she really finds out, I mean really, she is going to destroy us –

VICTOR. Clear up.

ANDRIUS. I will. Fine. Your hanky.

VICTOR. Keep it.

ANITA *re-enters. Silence.*

ANITA. Did I ever give you my CV? Don't think so. Okay, here it is: born in a boringly respectable home. Dad on the boats, on the rigs, now he's on incapacity benefit. Mum, a cleaner, paid cash in hand, died of breast cancer. Law-abiding, dole-dodging, ordinary people. Got my GCSEs and my Highers, did an extension course in Management which was bollocks, never been further afield than Portugal. That's me. Hardly worldy-wise. But no fool neither.

I know we're taking a liberal approach to the law here; I know our workers don't swan in on Eurostar, don't breeze through customs with a carefree smile; I know most of the

money we make'll not pass through the hands of Inland
Revenue. And I can't even believe I am saying this, even as I
say it: I know what's going on.

And maybe I am mad, but I trust you to do this the way it has
to be done, right. 'Cos I know for a fact it'll happen whether
we do it or not and I guess I'm naïve enough to believe you
care more, 'cos you know more, 'cos you've been where
these guys have been. And if we can do this better, cleaner
and get a roof over our heads and have a wee laugh along the
way, you know, I am totally utterly with you.

But if you abuse my trust – if you make this something dirty,
something ugly, something cruel – I will walk out and I will
not look back. Yeah?

So stick me on your letterhead, your website, your whatever.
'Cos the real question isn't, 'What do I know?', but, 'What
does Grimmer know?'

VICTOR. What he needs to.

ANDRIUS. More than you think.

VICTOR. If Grimmer make money, if they make money, if
everyone make money and they will make money, nobody
care how! So, we can shit in his soup, okay, but we lay on
the pepper and sour cream.

Okay, six months, drop Grimmer, gone; he sort our papers –

ALEXEI. Slowly –

VICTOR. Sure, sure, he's test us –

ANDRIUS. Six months I go home, buy up Kaunas –

VICTOR. I stay. I build something here.

When British people wake up, whenever whoever wants to
work this land gets to work this land, for week, month, year,
when real freedom of capital, freedom of labour then, I have
built this ready and waiting and we come into sunlight and
show our hands and they are clean.

GRIMMER *has entered.*

GRIMMER. Not changed them locks then? I would.

He puts his key on the table.

Brings back memories, this, though; started out in Lynn, trainee engineer, farming implements.

Dear old Dad went in with me on this, I think we paid, what was it, five grand, something silly.

One point had it lined up for my lad, Danny, but no, off to uni and all this's, what, provincial, right. It's all living in London and working on the telly for that lot.

Yeah, you've made it nice, you've made it home.

Pause.

VICTOR. We have – toast. Come in. Sit down, come in –

GRIMMER. Oh, the hub, right. Very impressive, all these pictures, maps. All these lines.

Ah, Moldavia. Your neck of the woods, Alexei?

Bit of a basket-case, they say. Makes Wales look like Monaco. He's still pissed at me, look at him, bless him.

No need to gawp at me, this is a friendly.

Christmas cards. Here.

Hands out to ALEXEI *and* VICTOR.

Don't open them and embarrass me. Little something in there. Meeting with a lawyer, date, time.

What was that about a toast, Victor? Bloody freezing out there. Wind from the Urals, is it? Certainly up your Urals. I just came to say I am very pleased; positive reports, phone's always ringing, good stuff.

More of the same to come, I hope.

VICTOR. Get another glass, Alexei.

GRIMMER. What's this then? Fakenham? Do I know about Fakenham?

VICTOR. Who took the call?

ANDRIUS. Me. Very recent.

GRIMMER. Fifteen in Fakenham. We got fifteen in there, have we?

VICTOR. Sure. Fifteen in Fakenham.

GRIMMER. And I thought we were at capacity.

ALEXEI has recharged the glasses.

VICTOR. You toast, Mr Grimmer.

GRIMMER. No, I wouldn't know how. I just drink it, I let you chaps do the national customs.

Yeah, it's really cosy in here, all hugger-mugger.

Festive. Your health!

VICTOR. Second toast. Anita, your shout.

ANITA. Oh, okay. To the Ukraine!

VICTOR. Yes!

ANDRIUS. I just smile.

VICTOR. Second.

ANITA. To… making honest money!

ALEXEI. Yes.

ANITA. To – friendship. Between nations.

She drinks three vodkas in a row.

GRIMMER. Puts it away like a native.

ALEXEI. Drink like a man.

ANITA. You've not seen me. This stuff is excellent.

You've not seen nothing yet.

Blackout.

End of Act Two.

ACT THREE

Scene One

A conservatory opening out onto a garden in a new house on the outskirts of King's Lynn; the following autumn. The room is large, chiefly empty; an entrance right leading into the house is an open arch masked by plastic; there's a halogen light lighting the spaces on both sides; through the gap an equally vacant living room is partially evident; stage left French windows open out onto a garden; there are sounds of work going on outside. Upstage, a trestle table with a row of bottles – whisky, vodka, champagne, beer, glasses. Next to it a camping table with a tablecloth loaded with Ukrainian food: smoked sausages, sour cream, salads, cold pancakes. Boxes of unpacked IKEA flat-pack furniture are draped in the corner under a sheet. A naked lightbulb hangs from the ceiling; wiring hangs from unplastered walls. There are some perfunctory attempts at decoration; a reproduction of an Ikon with streamers round it on the back wall; a large sheet of designer's paper with a groundplan of the house and elsewhere the garden. It's 7.30 in the evening.

VICTOR, in a new suit, no tie, stands with his wife, TANYA, opening up a bottle of champagne, serving drinks to ALEXEI and ANITA, who are dressed casually, as if caught in the middle of an activity; ALEXEI's hand is bandaged.

VICTOR. Champagne from Ukraine!

TANYA. From Yalta.

VICTOR. It's hot in Yalta. Vines flourish. One for Andrius? Where is he?

ALEXEI. Said he'd be here seven, seven-thirty.

VICTOR. Can't hold toast, it'll go flat. Anita, toast.

TANYA. You ask her?

ANITA. I'd prefer not to.

TANYA. Wish English was better. My, my –

ANITA. Better than my Russian.

TANYA. You learn Russian? Why?

Why English woman speak Russian?

ANITA. I'm Scottish, actually. From Scotland.

Pause.

VICTOR. Okay, I make toast. To coming home.

TANYA. Good.

ALEXEI. Very good.

They drink, rather meditatively. They speak in Russian.
ANITA *wanders off into the garden.*

VICTOR. We met in Yalta.

TANYA. You know Crimea, Alexei?

ALEXEI. No. I went to Odessa once.

TANYA. Yalta; and I was young, naïve. You were slim.

VICTOR. The Greek introduced us.

TANYA. Ah, the Greek, okay. Andreas.

VICTOR. He had this fishing smack, used to set out at night,
cross the Black Sea, down to Turkey –

TANYA. – come back with denims, videos, cigarettes –

VICTOR. Marlboros – nobody smoked Marlboros in Ukraine
then, did they – ?

TANYA. Half in Victor's Lada, half in bags on trains up to
Kiev, to Lviv, to Kharkiv –

VICTOR. She used to flog them on the night train to Kiev –

TANYA. Yes, God, yes, on the night train. Dodging inspectors,
bribing the carriage ladies –

VICTOR (*laughs*). The Greek was obsessed with Led Zep.
Pirate CDs from Germany; Zep One, Two, Three, Four –

TANYA. 'Houses of the Holy', 'Physical Graffiti' –

VICTOR. Exactly – what was it: 'The Song Remains the Same'.

Pause.

Another life.

TANYA. Hard times.

ALEXEI. Living on barter.

VICTOR. You could make money but you had to be fast.

TANYA. 'Primitive Accumulation.'

VICTOR. No Marxist bollocks, please, Tanjevska.

ALEXEI. You don't like Marx?

VICTOR. My old man used to spout Marx at me, after a good long bender: 'To each according to their needs, lad.' Stupid old lush.

TANYA. His dad was the last true believer.

VICTOR. Look what it got him. Liver like an eggplant and a beggar's pension.

Pause.

TANYA. How was it for you, Alexei? Perestroika?

ALEXEI. Oh. Pretty shit to be honest.

I was in Afghanistan.

TANYA. Oh, you poor lamb. Mind you, we had to live on my bread and pickled cabbage.

VICTOR. Didn't see meat in a year.

TANYA. What was that joke about the dogs, you know, about the space dogs, Strelka and – you remember Strelka – and Belka, yeah, Strelka asks Belka, 'So – (I can't tell jokes) so, (says Strelka) how's things for you under perestroika?' And Belka says – hang on, let me get this right – Belka says, 'Good and bad.' 'Good and bad?' says Strelka, 'How can this be?'

VICTOR. Get on with it!

TANYA. Alright, so Belka says, 'Good, good – they took away my chain; but bad, 'cos they don't feed me any more.'

She laughs loudly. ANITA *has wandered back in again with flowers behind her back.*

Good time – for you?

ANITA. What? When?

VICTOR. Perestroika. Late '80s, early '90s.

TANYA. Good time for you?

ANITA. Fine. I was, y'know, at primary school.

Pause. VICTOR *surveys the food table.*

VICTOR. No meat then, but now look at the spread. Vanneki, black bread, pirogi, smetana. Excellent work, Alexei, excellent –

ANITA. It was me, actually.

VICTOR. How?

ANITA. Located a wholesaler. On the web.

TANYA. She not make this?

ANITA. You joking, can't cook to save my life –

VICTOR. You cooked me pizza.

TANYA. She cook for you?

VICTOR. On one occasion.

ANITA. Stuck a pizza in the microwave. Hardly Nigella.

TANYA. What?

ANITA. Not cooking, really.

(*Re: the flowers.*) I got you these, Victor – Tanya too, I guess. To remind you – of home.

TANYA *won't take them.*

TANYA. I cannot take –

ANITA. Wee gift –

TANYA (*in Russian*). Victor, look, there's four.

VICTOR (*in Russian*). Don't be stupid.

TANYA (*in Russian*). You know it's bad luck –

VICTOR (*in Russian*). I'll take one away, look.

He does, then hands them to TANYA.

ANITA. Have I offended her or something?

VICTOR. Ukraine bullshit. Even numbers: bad luck. Put them in water, then. Tanya. Quickly.

TANYA. Where?

VICTOR. The kitchen, there. Be grateful, be nice, this is my friend.

TANYA goes; VICTOR *hands a single flower back to* ANITA.

One too many.

ANITA. Oh. Fine. My mistake.

ANITA strips the flower, absent-mindedly, of its petals.

VICTOR. I'm sweating, it's hot, October and hot.

Let's open these –

(*He opens the glass doors; shouts.*) Serhei! Put the mulch here, on the beds there, good; clear out the pines, grub them up.

See the sea, Anita. Yes? North Sea.

ANITA. Bought yourself a nice wee view.

VICTOR. Finish the champagne.

ANITA. Too sweet for me.

VICTOR. You look – amazing.

ANITA. No, I'm not dressed right. Didn't expect a party.

He goes to kiss her; she backs off.

Get off.

Pause.

VICTOR. Sorry – about Tanya. She's – confused.

ANITA. I bet.

VICTOR. Must be very big – shock.

ANITA. What – that you have a wife and children?

That you intend to settle them in this house, that presumably's been built for them?

It's food for thought.

VICTOR. Yes, I handle this badly.

ANITA. You did say you had business to attend to, but I guess you could have been a wee bit more explicit.

TANYA (*off, in Russian*). There's no water.

VICTOR. Of course there's water.

VICTOR goes off.

ANITA. She's very pretty.

ALEXEI. Sure.

ANITA. Prettier than me.

ALEXEI. You are very pretty also.

ANITA. She's got the bigger tits, though.

ALEXEI. Different style.

ANITA. Blonde, of course.

ALEXEI. All Ukrainian women are blonde.

ANITA. Not from a bottle, neither.

ALEXEI. Ukrainian women, Russian women, start good-looking, tits, make-up, good skin, okay, then they become their mothers – fat, tits down here, face lines, bad teeth. It's different.

ANITA. No, no, they're women like they used to be, right?

Like they ought to be. Can smell the perfume from here. Guess you knew about her?

ALEXEI *shrugs*.

Course you did. God, he's got a few surprises up his sleeve. Not as many as us though, hey? How they doin'? They gonna – live, those boys?

ALEXEI. Sure.

ANITA. Ah, lucked out then.

She lights up a cigarette.

ALEXEI. No smoking – in house.

ANITA. Oh, right.

She stands at the window, smoking.

ALEXEI. Could not contact you. All day. I tried phone.

ANITA. I switched it off.

ALEXEI. I see.

ANITA. Had to think.

ALEXEI. Yes. Don't think too much.

ANITA. Don't you tell me what to do with my own mind! We better tell him.

ALEXEI. I tell him. When Tanya –

ANITA. Let me tell him later.

ALEXEI. Why?

ANITA. Let him have his moment.

Let her think it's all real and solid, like we all did.

VICTOR *re-enters tying his tie;* ANITA *stubs out her cigarette.*

VICTOR. Looks like IKEA in there, Alexei.

ALEXEI. Furniture arrived late.

VICTOR. Why didn't you pick it up yourself?

ALEXEI. Been busy.

VICTOR. What happened with the builders?

ALEXEI. English contractor. Got other work.

VICTOR. We pay cash in hand. Should get our people on it. You try put money in local economy! Okay. Andrius still not here?

ALEXEI. I don't know. I text him. No answer.

VICTOR. Someone smoking?

(*Shouts out of the window; in Russian.*) This is non-smoking site, okay?

(*To* ANITA.) Did I say you look beautiful?

ANITA. Oh, 'amazing' – but not beautiful.

I'll go and pack my stuff.

VICTOR. What?

ANITA. Check in a Travelodge. There's stuff, urgent stuff we need to –

VICTOR. Tanya and I –we talk about when would be right, to come, I said not now, she, she is very – persuasive. (*Laughs.*) This is – try-out – and for you, this is not how I intend you two, you know, to – meet.

ANITA. It's okay, Victor. We're very adult in this country. We honestly don't feel certain out-of-date emotions, the sort of things people, women feel in films, say, jealousy, humiliation, that's all behind us. I'll go pack.

She goes.

VICTOR. Anita!

She's weird, she's changed. Even in a week.

ALEXEI. Don't let her leave.

VICTOR. She won't leave, she's just – And you, you look tired, brother.

ALEXEI. A little.

VICTOR. And you're scruffy.

Go to my bedroom, there are suits in the wardrobe, shave – Have you slept even?

Why are you hiding your hand?

ALEXEI. I – burnt – it.

VICTOR. You're a figure of authority, Alexei.

I can't mother you, friend. Oh, and your breath smells of onions. Jesus, clean your teeth, yeah?

Pause.

Have I made a mistake? Your honest answer.

ALEXEI. She got a return flight?

VICTOR. She's on an open ticket.

ALEXEI. Victor, I do not consider this to be wise.

VICTOR. Well, I'm not fucking wise. I'm not patient enough! Anita must have known – Look at me, a good-looking guy in his forties, would I not have a wife? I'm not a queer, clearly.

ALEXEI. It's not about Tanya.

VICTOR. I said to Tanya I'd missed her every second, every hour, I said to her, 'Everything I have done in this country has been to get to this moment' – and I believe that to be the case.

But, yes, it feels… different than I imagined it. She, she looks different than I remember.

ALEXEI. Victor, there's a situation.

VICTOR. Go and wash up, you're in your work clothes, take a shower, there are three showers.

ALEXEI. Only two working.

VICTOR. Fucking English plumbers, Jesus.

ALEXEI *goes*. VICTOR *is alone*.

(*Shouts*.) Take out that tree, it's screening the view, yeah, the dwarf pine.

Sound of a saw, off. TANYA *enters*.

TANYA. This house is so big.

VICTOR. Of course it's big.

TANYA. I have never seen such a big house.

VICTOR. It's not especially big. For this country.

I'd say it's modest. For this country.

Five bedrooms. You get houses with six, seven.

TANYA. Five bedrooms. Who's going to sleep in all these beds?

VICTOR. We'll have guests, I work here, this is our office, our life –

TANYA. So many bedrooms for a small family.

VICTOR. One for each of the girls.

TANYA. They like being together, they've always shared rooms.

VICTOR. They'll like the new privacy.

TANYA. Privacy? They'll be lonely.

VICTOR. Yes, space to be alone. To wash and bathe alone.

TANYA. They're sisters, Victor!

VICTOR. But as they grow older. Each of us has our own bathroom. Our own shower. You'll never have to wait for a shower ever again.

TANYA. A bathroom each, too? All showering at once, all alone in our separate showers, good God it's crazy, Victor.

VICTOR. No, it's not crazy, it's – en suite.

TANYA. And who'll clean these many, many bathrooms?

VICTOR. You're fixating on details –

TANYA. But they'll need cleaning, the tiles, the floors, all the glass, I have never seen so much glass, the heat must fly straight out of the house, it's profligate.

VICTOR. It's not a problem. I'll get in a girl.

TANYA. And who'll pay for your girl? We don't have maids, this is not Chekhov!

VICTOR. It's strange for you, I know. To walk into a dream. But it's not a dream, you're awake, these things that you see around you are real, yes, everything is real and everything is paid for.

He holds her.

You liked the kitchen at least?

TANYA. Nice, glass, glass cupboards, glass partitions. Very nice. Light. The sea.

VICTOR. Kept thinking about you in that galley kitchen, yeah, drawers there, here, the sour stink of gas, no window, strip light, a cage; all of us round that pathetic little pull-down table; getting food on our laps; two hobs, the hours it took to cook anything, to find anything, dirty dishes stacked in the sink.

TANYA. The cupboards are so high up.

I can't possibly reach them.

VICTOR. They're capacious! They have capacity and –

TANYA. Truly capacious. You could fit your mother in them. Victor, even the fridge is taller than me.

How can I reach things at the back of that fridge? I'd need arms as long as a man's.

I could lose myself in that fridge.

She bursts out laughing.

Isn't it crazy, though? In a way?

VICTOR. Are you laughing at me?

She kisses him.

TANYA. Victor, love. When are we going home?

VICTOR. What?

TANYA. Surely now, with all this you can pay off my cousins.

VICTOR. No, Tanya – no –

TANYA. They're building a warehouse on the factory site – Tesco! Unbelievable. The fire's forgiven, the fire raised the value of the site, they say they're grateful to you. Just get them their money with some token interest, what – sell this house – they always said, none of it is personal, it's business, 'primitive accumulation'–

VICTOR. You've understood nothing!

Pause.

I was running a legitimate business –

TANYA. You borrowed their money, Victor.

VICTOR. I needed capital, sure, where else do I go, to the bank? The interest was extortionate – they were milking us!

TANYA. Negotiate it down.

VICTOR. Negotiate with thieves?

TANYA. Come on, Victor, you could have sold up, made a little money, moved on.

VICTOR. You see, you don't even see it!

TANYA. They go through the motions – you oblige. It stops.

VICTOR. No, it never stops, never, it's a way of life.

TANYA. I didn't like them turning up at the school, scaring the girls, that was nasty; but after you left, it was just the odd call in the middle of the night.

VICTOR. You never submit to threats, never –

TANYA. You always have to challenge things!

It's how it works, Vitya, how we always did it, look at the Greek, you pay people, a little payment, a tax, really, a tax where there's no government to take tax, it's fair, it works, but no, no, you had to challenge it, you were too clean –

VICTOR. I am not a fucking serf, okay, not a serf crawling about under some mafia horsewhip!

TANYA. – so damn smart you have to fly halfway across the Earth, so clever we have to flee what we know, what we love, to come finally, to come here, away from everything we know and care about, my God –

VICTOR. Your mind is the mind of a thief!

TANYA. What did you say to me?

VICTOR. But then, this is us, our problem, we don't believe in justice, ruled by thieves all our lives, made into thieves, all of us, farmers filching fodder, workers nicking parts, doctors, drugs, drivers, petrol, thieves stealing from thieves! In this country there's law.

Here, life's in your hands, all this here is just one step on a long, long ladder, one step on a ladder of your own making!

Pause.

TANYA. You could always talk up a storm.

VICTOR. You could always imagine. That's why you went for me, not some prick sloping round a machine shop.

TANYA. Nothing, nothing from you, days, months, silence.

VICTOR. I was not free… I mean, I was in a blur.

TANYA. The girls? I could hardly bear to leave them, I promised them I'd be no longer than a week, I won't stay longer.

VICTOR. The girls'll thrive here, they'll flourish here.

TANYA. But we don't want this, Vitya, we want you!

And anyway, this, this, they will never permit you to live like this! You're dreaming again!

Silence. VICTOR *makes a drink.*

VICTOR. There's some clothes in the bedroom.

TANYA. What?

VICTOR. You can change into them. Have a shower –

TANYA. I am ready as I can be.

VICTOR. Okay. But… your face. The make-up's too…

TANYA. My face?

VICTOR. You need less here, round the eyes.

Look at English women.

TANYA. I do. They look like tramps.

VICTOR. As I say, clothes in the bedroom.

TANYA. I bought this outfit new in Kiev.

VICTOR. I want you to look right.

TANYA. Oh, so I look funny to you.

VICTOR. No, not to me, no –

TANYA. What, so no make-up, no, off with which of my clothes – my blouse, my jewels you bought me – my St Christopher, my ring maybe, where's yours by the way?

VICTOR. It was stolen – by Turks –

TANYA. And you haven't replaced it? I would have replaced it with the first kopek I earned.

VICTOR. Go, get changed, now, get changed.

ALEXEI has entered in a suit.

There's no time for childishness, Tanya.

She goes off.

I need to drink, and now. Join me.

ALEXEI. I've had sufficient.

VICTOR. You haven't begun. Whisky. Here. Quick one. Your suit's baggy at the waist, pull the belt in, Jesus, must I do it all myself. Drink.

VICTOR gets him a drink from the bar.

ALEXEI. Victor, there is a serious situation –

VICTOR. What do you want? We've got the works.

ALEXEI. I don't care.

VICTOR. Cocktails, yes, yes, come on.

He mixes him a drink.

Down it, down it.

ALEXEI *does.*

ALEXEI. Fuck!

VICTOR. You secured the tulips, the Spalding people?

ALEXEI. Yes.

VICTOR. Good, more like it, good. Drink more.

He does.

We cleared up the Western Union thing?

ALEXEI. Yes. Payments over ten thousand need multiple payees, multiple –

VICTOR. And Davies extended the winter contract, okay?

ALEXEI. I don't know, Andrius –

VICTOR. Andrius, Andrius, he should never have been put in charge of the money. He says, 'Go overground, get into the official economy', but I don't trust the people he's talking to, they smell like Grimmer –

ALEXEI. Victor, there's been an accident.

VICTOR. What?

ALEXEI. A fire.

VICTOR. What did you say?

Pause.

ALEXEI. The key thing you always say is appropriate response, I mean, I responded okay; lost the house, okay, got pretty much everyone out of the house – It had to happen, we've been fortunate to get this far without – fatalities –

VICTOR. Fatalities? Wait, stop and begin over.

ALEXEI. I lock them in from the outside maybe, maybe I should
think about that – but you keep the curfew then and, and you
leave a key with a responsible party, always, always –

VICTOR. You're not making sense so shut up, shut up and start
– making sense –

Pause.

ALEXEI. Cold Harbour Farm; the Moldovan kids. With the –
the –

VICTOR. The wiring?

ALEXEI. Gutted. Totally gutted.

VICTOR. No.

Pause.

No. How, how many did we – ?

ALEXEI. Twenty-five.

VICTOR. No. No we weren't going to do that, we agreed only
under – twenty? Two-up, two-down – no, three storeys –

ALEXEI. Last batch from Misha, there were ten stowaways,
and there was demand, plenty of demand, but capacity was a
problem –

VICTOR. Did I know this?

ALEXEI. You said for a week maybe and, okay, it's been longer
and they were happy with it, mainly lads, some girls, stuck
the girls in the roof to keep them, you know, private from the
lads, you know these boys, Victor, fuck anything in knickers.

VICTOR. Oh God. How many?

ALEXEI. I got twenty-four out, twenty-four out of twenty-five,
yes. Ground floor, a bit asphyxiated, smoke; first floor, burns,
second-degree mainly; attic, serious – burns.

Pause.

VICTOR. No one called the – what, the – fire station.

ALEXEI. No phones, no English, no one for miles, one boy jumped, broke his legs, tried to reach me – Oh, fuck – oh, I'm sorry, Victor, I –

ALEXEI *sits on the floor and covers his face.*

VICTOR. This is a catastrophe.

ALEXEI. I am one hundred per cent culpable.

VICTOR. No, no, this is a judgement.

ALEXEI. Wires going into tobacco tins, you'd got shocks from the light fixtures, one kid had a kettle, fuck knows where from –

VICTOR. Who was left in there?

ALEXEI. A girl, an ignorant lump of a girl – from Dnestrovski. Eighteen or so.

VICTOR. A girl. What happened to her?

ALEXEI. Don't know. The others got down before the stairs went. Dunno. Passed out?

VICTOR. She burned?

ALEXEI *nods; pause.*

You know her name?

ALEXEI *shakes his head.*

A girl. Eighteen.

ALEXEI *nods.*

So now we're killers.

ALEXEI. The kids were throwing their things out the windows, I mean, what did they have anyway, they had nothing like we had nothing, you had nothing.

Silence.

VICTOR. Oh God. Oh God.

VICTOR *laboriously takes off his jacket, unravels his tie.*

It's done.

ALEXEI. Yes.

VICTOR. It's done.

ALEXEI. Yes.

VICTOR. Every day it happens. Those Poles caught in a bailer, that van of Kurds, we almost, you nearly killed me, remember – Did Grimmer go to court? No.

ALEXEI. Yeah. Every day.

VICTOR. The other kids, the ones who got out.

ALEXEI. All illegals. I briefed them. Said we'd get them home free if they wished to go.

No one wanted to go, not one. You'd have been proud. Nobody knew her. The girl.

VICTOR. Good, good for them, good.

ALEXEI. But Anita, Victor.

ANITA *enters with* TANYA; ANITA *is in the sharpest of business clothes with a bag;* TANYA *looks uncomfortable in her new clothes.*

VICTOR. Alexei, look, look out for Andrius, he should be –

ALEXEI *goes.*

TANYA (*in Russian*). Who is this woman, truly, Vitya?

ANITA. Is she asking who I am? You didn't say?

Head of liaison, would you call it that, Victor, did we ever have a job description written out?

VICTOR. Anita is at the – centre of – what we do.

TANYA (*in Russian*). Speak in Russian. Don't speak in English in her presence. If she's your secretary, why's she dressed like a tart? Look at this lipstick.

I took off my make-up.

VICTOR. Yes, you're pale, yes. I can't see you.

ANITA. Why did she change? She looked so sweet before.

TANYA (*in Russian*). I'm not an idiot, Vitya. The way she watches you.

ANITA. You've kept your figure, Tanya.

VICTOR. You're wearing trousers, good. Yes, they suit you.

TANYA (*in Russian*). Whatever she does for you I can do for you.

VICTOR. I like everything fine, as it is, as it was.

ANITA. This is getting private now? Should I piss off?

TANYA (*in Russian*). Tell me everything and everything will be forgiven.

ALEXEI *comes back in*.

ALEXEI. Andrius's here.

VICTOR. At last.

ALEXEI. With Grimmer.

VICTOR. What?

ALEXEI. He came in Grimmer's car.

VICTOR. Grimmer?

ALEXEI. Yes.

Pause.

VICTOR. Okay. Get them drinks. Take them in the garden. Wait. Get the kids to clear up there, he doesn't know about – Wait –

(*Shouts.*) Okay, that's fine, that's – Serhei, drive them, drive them back, lead them. (*To* ALEXEI.) Keep Grimmer out front, show him the cars, the house, introduce him to Tanya. Tanya, I need you to meet this guy – Fuck, I'm not ready – Anita, don't go, let's talk – Wait – I'll –

(*Shouts, stumbling out through the windows to the garden.*) Serhei, clear them off, wait I'll help with the – There should be lights on, lights on in the garden lighting up the path, where are the lights?

ALEXEI *heads out to the front. The women are alone.*

ANITA. I didn't know about you.

TANYA. Yes you did.

Pause.

ANITA. Well, mebbe I did – know – and like so many other things you know, I chose not to… think about it.

TANYA. What are you saying?

ANITA. He lied. About you.

TANYA. Victor not lie.

ANITA. No, he's not a liar, he's a storyteller.

Bedded on a fucking story, me. Now he's brought you over on a story. Christ knows the stories are good.

But there are too many of them and they don't fit together.

ALEXEI *comes back to the door.*

ALEXEI. Tanya.

TANYA (*to* ANITA, *in Russian*). I have nothing to say to you, bitch.

She joins ALEXEI *at the door.*

ANITA. Don't need an interpreter for that.

VICTOR *returns from the garden, soil on his hands.*

VICTOR. Timer switch – broken. Security light comes on fine. Timer's – faulty.

He tries to wipe off the soil, it's on his shirt.

ANITA. I enjoyed sleeping here while you were away. The views. The birds – curlews, are they? With the beaks? Yeah. Curlews.

I was thinking when you got back, tonight, we would go for a walk and see 'em. I got you the food too, thought you'd be excited; and I was gonna suggest something. I had this stupid idea you could, I dunno, move into wholesale, retail, import –export. Y'see the kind of a silly bitch I am?

She starts to go.

VICTOR. Don't go –

ANITA. I don't think we should be alone now, do you?

He blocks her path.

I hope you're not going to try to kiss me again.

VICTOR. Just to see you, God. Makes me – hard.

ANITA. Don't be so – tacky.

He places her hand on his groin.

VICTOR. Feel how I feel for you.

ANITA. Oh God, very fucking clever.

Very big and clever.

VICTOR. Now, tell me I lie.

ANITA. Okay, give you a little pull and things are cool, right?
Mebbe your poor wee missus comes in.

Here, here – this what you're after, bit of fast work here, one
off the wrist, this what you want nice and hard on you, you
like it hard and fast and British –

VICTOR. Yes, yes –

ANITA. Do it yourself, you bastard.

She walks away.

VICTOR. God.

ANITA. You've got hands, haven't you?

They stand in silence; ANITA *cries.*

What was her name?

VICTOR. Who?

ANITA. 'Cos you'll need a name when you contact the
authorities.

You'll need a name for the funeral, right.

Pause.

VICTOR. I did not know her.

ANITA. Well, let's see, she'll have come from some ugly town,
somewhere I'll not have heard of. Arrived last week, dead of
night. Unplanned, Misha, is it Misha, Alexei's pal, yes, Misha
stuck her in a truck, probably, last-minute thing, nobody's
fault. She'll have paid, sure she paid, they pay, of course they
pay, a thousand euros, now where'd she get money like that,
the family, what are they, oh, maybe they own like a factory, a
sausage factory, mebbe, maybe they just lost this factory,
must have sold everything for her to come, that's a year's
wages at least; just a week here, she'll have seen a few things,
alright, poly-tunnels at night, cabbages under arclights, the
back of a number of minibuses, sleeping bag still stinking of
its last occupant, a hot, unventilated attic room, welcome to
freedom, well, you'd know about that welcome, Victor –

VICTOR. Yes.

ANITA. – long day, long night, but it'd be worth it, once she'd
paid you off, the truckers off, year of this, year's sweat down
the line she might be in credit but, hey, she didnae get to get
that far – did she – did she?

Pause.

VICTOR. It was an accident –

ANITA. Oh yeah, can't be helped. Manslaughter. Corporate
crime. What do you think? Magistrates' court. Slapped wrist.
Then, for you, deportation. For me, oh, I can plead all sorts
of mitigating shit.

VICTOR. Nothing connects the house to you.

ANITA. No, no, fair dos, I did warn you, I did that much well,
I'm the human being, right?

VICTOR. You are kind.

ANITA. Oh aye, kind.

I went there this afternoon. Still smoking.

It's a crime scene, Victor. You should take a look. They're
taking their time. You should see how they work. They're

good at their jobs. Somewhere in all the shit and ash our names are waiting to be found.

VICTOR. She came here of her own free will –

ANITA. Oh, shut up.

VICTOR. She came to earn money to live a little better –

ANITA. Shut up –

VICTOR. And, and she was free to go, free to go at any time, free.

ANITA. Oh right, free? What, hobbled with some humungous debt? Not a word of English. Free? What, like you were?

VICTOR. Fundamentally free, yes. Free to come, free to work and free to return.

ANITA. You didn't seem too free back then.

VICTOR. I wonder did you ask her, her, no go to the others, the lucky ones –

ANITA. Burned, traumatised –

VICTOR. Go ask them what they prefer; to leave, or to stay?

ANITA. That's a false, lying question.

VICTOR. That's only question. Why did she die? Because she find work? This kill her? Work? No, Anita. Your law kills her. Lies kill her.

ANITA. Our laws could have saved her!

VICTOR. Your law want her back where she come, poor, for ever poor, far away as possible.

Still, she wish to come. Tell policeman this, waiting to send her back, and you, you all behind him, lined up, all of you, you want us, don't want us, cheap food, cheap people, but you don't know how it all gets to be so cheap, you dream, dream and your dreams kill people.

ANITA. God, you talk such lies.

VICTOR. Anita –

He tries to take her; she slaps him in the face.

ANITA. I'll hurt you.

VICTOR. You could not hurt me.

He tries again, she throws his drink in his face.

ANITA. Sorry – are you –

VICTOR. It's fine, fine –

ANITA. You okay?

VICTOR. Sure, sure.

He wipes his face with his shirt tails.

ANITA. Because I cannae – I cannae be – involved in this, honest I can't.

VICTOR. Of course, I will see you are not linked –

ANITA. No, Victor, no, it's worse than that – I'm going to the police!

Pause.

I've kept records, I'm coming clean, 'fessing up.

VICTOR. What?

ANITA. I said I would. Keep records. Of everything.

VICTOR. Anita, no, don't do this.

ANITA. I said, I did, I warned you, I told you.

VICTOR. I will take steps, contact family, arrange –

ANITA. No, it's too late for that. Too late. I'm scared now, truly.

VICTOR. You think you do this to me. You cannot.

You say this now but you will not. You are kind.

Voices approach from the garden.

ANITA. Oh, shit, shit, I'm all over the shop, shit.

I'm going. I really am going.

VICTOR. What must I change? You want Tanya go? Gone, gone.

ANITA. I'll give you an hour's grace.

VICTOR. No go home, come in morning.

ANITA. See, I'm not a criminal, I told you, not a criminal, never was! An hour, Victor.

>ANITA *goes out through the house*. ANDRIUS, GRIMMER, ALEXEI *enter;* TANYA *watches from outside, smoking; it's dark now but lights are on outside*.

ANDRIUS. Victor, good evening.

VICTOR. What?

TANYA (*in Russian*). You're hurt?

ANDRIUS. Yes, it's a fine evening out there.

GRIMMER. Cooling down. See clear to the Wash.

TANYA (*in Russian*). What happened to your shirt?

VICTOR (*in Russian*). Nothing.

>*Pause.*

ANDRIUS. Mike can't stay long.

>*Pause.*

VICTOR. Mike. Yes. Hello, hello. Fine, fine.

>Great. You came. Drink?

GRIMMER. I'm not drinking.

ANDRIUS. Mike has a meeting later.

VICTOR. Mike again!

GRIMMER. That's my name. Don't wear it out.

VICTOR. Kind of you to drop by.

GRIMMER. I was in the vicinity.

ANDRIUS. We needed to re-establish contact. Right?

ALEXEI (*in Russian*). You're a sick joke.

VICTOR. Keep it English.

GRIMMER. I'm nosey I am. Like to see what you're spending all your money on.

VICTOR. Invest in property.

ANDRIUS. My advice, Victor.

GRIMMER. Very wise.

VICTOR. Buy view. Clear everything, maximise view. Location is thing. Like your place, Mike.

You know view from Mike's garden, Andrius?

ANDRIUS. Of course. Ely Cathedral.

VICTOR. Ely Cathedral. British knew how to build back then. Built to last.

GRIMMER. Yeah, it's a lost art. These days, look at that –

He indicates wiring.

Well, standards are lower.

VICTOR. Will be covered up.

ANDRIUS. Polish builders, right?

VICTOR. English.

GRIMMER. Irish, more like.

Yeah, nice house potentially, but everything's rushed, there's no sense of craft, no one's sticking about. Like your garden – some nice ideas. Nice annuals. But no long-term vision. You get someone in?

VICTOR. Early stages.

GRIMMER. And all those lights, Victor, turn it down, please. It's a bit municipal, ain't it!

Pergola. Okay, better. Looking a little raw though, a bit naked. Needs a fast-grower.

VICTOR. I see. What you suggest?

GRIMMER. I tell you what's a real fast-grower, Russian vine. Boy, that goes fast. Mile-a-minute, we call it; real cheeky little thing; give it a foothold, next thing it's all over the shop. Perfect for immature gardens like yours.

VICTOR. Russian vine. Okay.

Pause. ANDRIUS *is giggling.*

ALEXEI (*in Russian*). Why are you laughing?

ANDRIUS. Sorry. Is nothing. Really.

Pause.

TANYA. Mr Grimmer, a drink, please. And for Andrius.

ANDRIUS. No thanks, I'm driving – Mike.

ALEXEI. You drink.

TANYA. Please, I feel ashamed, you must –

GRIMMER. Okay, go on then, a quickie. I'll have a gin and it.

TANYA *is at the bar.*

TANYA. Gin, gin. Okay. Gin. We don't have gin.

We have brandy, vodka, slivovitz, Scotch.

GRIMMER. I'll give it a miss, then.

TANYA. It's all the best, the best of everything.

GRIMMER. I fancied a gin.

TANYA. I make you tea?

GRIMMER. Tea? Little late in the day for tea, love.

TANYA. Food, then. Delicacies from – homeland.

GRIMMER. These your famous sausages, Victor?

He surveys them.

TANYA. Sausages, yes, Kovbasa we say, double-smoked, Lvivska, delicious from the west, garlic –

GRIMMER. No, I'm not hungry, thanks, love.

TANYA. Best, the very best of Ukrainian food.

GRIMMER. Yeah, bit of a tender tummy, darling.

TANYA (*in Russian*). These people are laughing at you, Vitya.

VICTOR. That's bad manners, Tanya.

TANYA (*in Russian*). These are your friends?

VICTOR. No, we speak English here.

TANYA (*in Russian*). Don't talk to me that way.

VICTOR. English!

TANYA *storms out to the garden, then smokes, watches.*

GRIMMER. Okay, let's cut the niceties.

First proposition, as of tonight, Andrius is working for me. Short notice, I know, but as I understand, there's no contract, and I can pay you off. How much?

ANDRIUS. To be honest, Victor, I have reached point where I need change.

GRIMMER. Very smart, alert sort of chap.

I think it's fair to say, stop me if I'm wrong, mate, but I think the whole of us, the whole community are feeling a bit rattled. By what you've done – I mean, we all have accidents but, well – rule number one, you look after your own. Right?

VICTOR. You told him.

ANDRIUS. I know you understand this is not personal. I have had very good time working with for Fast Labour. But we are companies, people move from employer to employer.

Normal.

ALEXEI. He told him.

GRIMMER. Well, Cold Harbour Farm's seen more action than a knocking shop. But things move on. It's like these new licences, you seen these yet?

He gets out a gangmasters licence.

Oh, you get yourself checked out with – what are they – the Licensing Authority; bit of a laugh, really – you show 'em your legits and your best-behaved paperwork and bingo –

you get your MOT. But you might find it harder – getting one of these. After last night.

ALEXEI (*in Russian*). They're pissing on us. Shitting in our mouths.

GRIMMER. Look, what do you want? I've bought the cheque-book. I like the look of the goods, proceed to checkout, yeah.

VICTOR. Andrius is big investment. Commercial secrets.

GRIMMER. He's gone, Victor. Off your books.

ANDRIUS. Mike's seen a lot of potential. In the Baltic states. Which is my patch, right?

GRIMMER. Well, you know you pay a little more but it's all out there, upfront, no – volatility – I mean, I like you Ukrainians, but the EU's getting bigger, Andrius here's been introducing me to places I had no idea about; Estonia, for one. I've tended to overlook Estonia.

ANDRIUS. Latvia.

GRIMMER. Course, you've got Romania coming on stream –

ANDRIUS. Bulgaria –

GRIMMER. Bulgaria, even, in the fullness of time, Turkey.

Why go to the dealer when you can get it at the chemist's? Keep it sweet, keep it legal.

I mean, if you can spare the guy, you're obviously doing great guns, if you can get on without me –

VICTOR. Fine. Okay. He's not worth much. What do you think, Alexei?

ALEXEI. Couple of kopeks.

VICTOR. If that.

ALEXEI. One kopek.

VICTOR. Gratis. Nothing. Take him for nothing.

ALEXEI. Not worth a piss in the Volga.

VICTOR. Not worth a Chechen's promise.

GRIMMER. Charming, charming. Let's go, lad.

VICTOR. No, no, let's shake on it. Come on, let's be… grown-up. Fine. You'll like working with each other. Mike will inspire you, Andrius. He inspire me, personally, from the start.

Always I ask, what would Mike do in my position?

GRIMMER. Yeah, but that's where there's a problem.

I'd never be in your position.

And you'd never be in mine.

VICTOR. No, no, we are the same, the same, Mike.

GRIMMER. I'll be honest with you, Victor.

I was extremely pissed at you for a long while.

You worked well for me, brought in a good calibre of migrant. That was all nice, that was as it should be. But you turned out to be very, how shall we say, arrogant. Presumptuous, is another word. You stole from me. I consider you a thief, actually. You stole my network, my connections, which I had built up through my own efforts, you stole my intellectual property.

VICTOR. Competition, Mike.

GRIMMER. Don't you ever, ever presume to call me by my Christian name, okay? Ever.

You don't actually know me. Okay?

VICTOR. Know you? I am you. Tonight we do what we always should – merge! Become one!

He embraces GRIMMER, *who shoves him away into the table of food;* VICTOR *falls on the floor amongst salads and sausages.*

GRIMMER. Merge, you bugger? Hey? Merge.

ALEXEI's *helping* VICTOR *up.*

You wanna look at this, here, lad – my phone, scroll through the fucking numbers there – what you got – Geoff Peters – you know Geoff? – course you don't, well then, Geoff's

what we call a procurer, for Sainsbury's, his turf's this whole
region – Geoff closes whole outfits like that in one phone
call, dead – and here's his number and, I don't need to say
this but why not, he's asked me on several occasions if I'd
like to work in retail and one day soon maybe I will – Look
there, boy, next number, Sir, yes, Sir Malcolm Pawson –
lives near me, Little Thetford, you know it, thought not –
Conservative MP for East Cambridgeshire, delightful man,
not a trace of haughtiness, farming background, he pops by,
he asks me for my opinion on rural matters, we play golf –
Who else, who else – Phil Preston, Chief Constable Preston
that is, my wife rides with Jenny, his missus, had them round
to dinner last Sunday, and it goes on, it goes on, you see,
yeah? No one foreign here, no one dodgy, no one at all – do
you see my point?

Dear God, you're a funny little fella, Victor – merge?

GRIMMER *starts laughing, wheezing, coughing.*

Excuse me, oh dear, oh God, you're a caution.

ANDRIUS. If I might be able to offer some small criticism of
your way of working, I think mostly a matter of style –
There's something maybe in the Slav temperament which
might be seen as greedy, maybe even thuggish, Alexei, yes,
something, volatile maybe –

VICTOR. Yeah, yeah, you pass unseen amongst them,
Andrius –

ANDRIUS. You know the cliché, peasants in supermarket,
right, want to eat everything, drink lovely drinks, wear bright
new clothes, thinking they're in heaven, because for so long
they had nothing, so now, now they deserve everything, in
their own way, on their own terms, right. I guess I'm starting
to find that – cliché – all too – true.

VICTOR*'s up on his feet with a fork in his hand.*

VICTOR (*in Russian*). Then go, be free. Flourish. What you
waiting for?

GRIMMER. Put it down, Victor, come on, lad – no need for –

VICTOR (*in Russian*). Fuck off and flourish. It's easier for you, Andrius. Europe wants you. It doesn't want us. But you, yes. You pass amongst them unrecognised.

GRIMMER. Put it down, mate – and this can end now.

VICTOR. Just another cunt from Europe.

ANDRIUS. You're a thief, Victor, finally.

You're working with thieves, with crooks.

ALEXEI *pulls* ANDRIUS *down into a clinch, they fall into the mess of food, rolling around in an ugly melee of spilled cream, crushed meat, spilled drink;* VICTOR *joins in, trying to pull off* ANDRIUS; GRIMMER *tries to extricate* ANDRIUS.

ALEXEI. Judas, you fucking Judas, you fucking –

GRIMMER. Get off him, get off him –

ALEXEI *punches* GRIMMER *in the gut; he crumples.* VICTOR*'s up,* ANDRIUS *on the floor, his face bloody. It's a short ugly brawl; they all break away, stunned, breathing hard.*

VICTOR. Alexei.

ALEXEI. Judas – fucking –

ANDRIUS. – bleeding – there's glass –

GRIMMER. Jesus –

VICTOR. Apologise, Alexei –

TANYA *rushes in.*

TANYA (*in Russian*). What are you doing?

VICTOR. Apologise, Alexei.

TANYA (*in Russian*). Shall I hurt them?

VICTOR (*in Russian*). Nothing, nothing –

TANYA (*in Russian*). I could hit him with this.

She shows a bottle.

GRIMMER. I do – not – fucking – believe this –

VICTOR. Mike, your suit, your face.

GRIMMER. Send you – send the – dry cleaner's bill. This – monkey – winded – me. God.

VICTOR. Look at you, Mike – you look funny –

VICTOR *is laughing*.

GRIMMER. Oh, you're a loose cannon, boy.

ALEXEI. Sorry, sorry, sorry.

TANYA (*in Russian*). Vitya. Are you hurt?

ANDRIUS (*in Russian*). Clumsy ignorant – fascists.

ALEXEI (*in Russian*). Sorry, Victor.

ANDRIUS *stands, dizzy and dishevelled*.

VICTOR. Like Dad. Drunk as a pig, shirt off, red face, lying in sick, never a free day, never a true day in his life. Belt cut me, cut, cut. I call him drunk, thief. Say life in west better. 'This is our life. This is our only life.'

GRIMMER. Yeah, your old dad got it about right; you've got an awful lot of catching up to do. Don't rate your chances. 'Cos frankly, I think you forgot. I think you forgot what you are.

ANDRIUS. It's what they do, Mike. It's what they always do.

GRIMMER. Come on, lad, leave this. This shit is over and done with.

GRIMMER *stumbles out*, ANDRIUS *follows*.

TANYA. Food everywhere. My God.

She starts to clean up.

ALEXEI. Sorry, Victor. My sincere apologies.

TANYA. That boy is a traitor. What is he? Lithuanian?

Always the first to betray us.

This is useless. What a mess.

VICTOR. How is Father?

TANYA. Vitya, they will go to the police.

VICTOR. God, what are we doing in this place?

Pause. They seem paralysed.

TANYA. There's papers in the house, right? Vitya?

Victor, I am not a fool, there are papers?

Forged papers, documents, false invoices?

Victor?

VICTOR. In another man's house.

TANYA. Alexei, there's incriminating – papers?

ALEXEI. Yes. Visas. Maps. Leases. Contracts. Yes.

TANYA. Get it all together, gather everything. Money, minutes, leases, maps.

Get it all in here. Alexei, get up, please, listen to me: all the paperwork.

ALEXEI goes off.

Now listen to me, Victor, that man will go to the police. The police will come here and you will be arrested and I will be deported, so, so we must get up and we must go home, Vitya. I'll drive. There's petrol in the car?

VICTOR. It was the Greek. The Greek got us into this.

TANYA. We'll go home. Go where we know the rules.

VICTOR. Crossing the Black Sea at night.

TANYA. Things have changed at home, really. They are changing.

He suddenly looks at her.

VICTOR. We'll never change. We're the world's trash.

I mean, did we choose our country? I don't think so. Did we say, yes, these flooded mines are mine, yes, these marshes glowing with radium are my fucking birthright? We had no choice.

TANYA. I don't know, I don't care about that. Maybe we sell
    this house somehow? Maybe that woman could sell it, sell it
    and, what, take a percentage – We could take some of it, sell
    some of it, we could drive, yes, if we drive we can take –
    through the tunnel, there's a tunnel we could drive through
    now –

    ALEXEI has sorted out heaps of papers.

ALEXEI. You want these burned? Victor.

    Here – invoices, ID papers, err – contracts – Victor? Tanya?

TANYA. Yes, burn it all. Out there. On the terrace.

ALEXEI. Really?

TANYA. There isn't time for discussion.

ALEXEI. Victor?

    VICTOR shrugs; ALEXEI goes out.

TANYA. I mean, no one checks you when you leave, right? No,
    we don't need these rooms.

    We don't need showers and cookers and televisions, we
    never needed these things before.

VICTOR. What is it, this feeling, you know, how everything,
    everything pushes you further and further from who you are,
    what is the word for that?

TANYA. These were never our needs. We're simple people.
    Vitya, you're a fundamentally simple person.

    *Fire is visible outside; ALEXEI troops in, fetches more
    documents.*

    Good, Alexei, good. Burn everything.

VICTOR. Burning names. All the names.

    Where'll they go now?

TANYA. Come on, they're tough kids, they'll be okay, they'll
    fend for themselves. You did.

VICTOR. Out there, what, two hundred-odd – names.

Alexei, call them up, call them all up, the workers. Forewarned they can do what you did.

ALEXEI *comes through*.

Alexei, call up every hostel, every caravan.

ALEXEI. Yeah, okay, I'll get Serhei on it.

Takes his phone out.

(*On the phone*.) Serhei? Yeah I know. Listen, listen – it's over.

VICTOR. Scatter the whole thing. Break the whole thing up.

ALEXEI. Serhei, call Yuri. Call Marya. Call, err, Marek.

VICTOR. In other people's houses, caravans, houses. Tired out from other people's work. Get them the money.

TANYA. No, we'll need the money, Vitya.

ALEXEI (*going out*). No forwarding addresses, nothing.

Yeah, be vague about money.

TANYA. Okay, if they take us we deny it, deny everything.

If they take us, we're one of them. This house is just a house. There are no papers. There'll be no money.

ALEXEI *comes in with plastic bags full of money.*

ALEXEI. No, I didn't get to offload the take.

There's a week's worth, more.

VICTOR. Alexei, yes. So take the money to them.

Take them all the money.

TANYA. We'll need it.

She takes some; he snatches the rest away.

VICTOR. Give them what they earned.

TANYA. Vitya, don't be a child.

VICTOR. Those kids, with the burns. Yeah? Compensation. Here, it's not our money, right. The Moldovans, the Bessarabians, the Belarussians, the Transdniestrians.

TANYA. Victor, please be serious.

VICTOR. It's not our money, love. None of it.

And you as well, mate.

Take, what, as much as you need.

But you distribute the rest. To each according to their needs, right?

ALEXEI. Okay, right – you –

VICTOR. This is what we have to do.

ALEXEI. Right. But do I come back here?

VICTOR. Take the van, take whoever you can fit in the van, flog the van. Work for someone else. Go home. Or stay. Drive. Let this burn.

ALEXEI. Well, okay. Okay. Good luck. It's good to be busy again. I'm sober. Good luck, brother.

He embraces VICTOR*; he's in tears.*

VICTOR. To each according to their needs, Alexei.

ALEXEI *nods; goes.* VICTOR *and* TANYA *are alone.*

TANYA. So you go home poorer than you left.

VICTOR. It's not my money, you know.

TANYA. Oh God, you stupid bastard, Victor, you stupid stupid child.

He goes to touch her; she shrugs him away.

How do we switch off the lights in the garden? They attract attention. That fire. No curtains. We must be visible for miles in here. Let's switch off the lights.

She plunges the room into darkness.

Okay. That's better. You should eat. Given we've – And then we should –

She gives him some sausage; takes one herself.

Ah, look at me, look, my hands are shaking, look, I'm in shock. Eat.

She eats.

Here, kovbasa, have some. It's pretty good.

VICTOR *eats*.

Yeah, not bad at all.

VICTOR. Yes. Yes. God – that's good.

TANYA. Yes. Tastes of home.

They eat in silence.

VICTOR. Kovbasa.

TANYA. Yes.

VICTOR. As good as ours.

TANYA. I don't think so.

They eat.

VICTOR. All I ever wanted was to fill people's bellies.

They eat more.

Remember, when we recruited for fifty jobs, do you remember –

TANYA. God, yes. All the women. Jesus.

VICTOR. Three hundred – you remember? Hungry – for work.

TANYA. A line round the block.

VICTOR. For fifty jobs. How do you choose?

TANYA. Here. Finish it. I'll pack the car.

She gets up.

VICTOR. Wait. And what did you say, Tanyevska?

TANYA. I honestly don't remember, love.

VICTOR. You said, 'Look at their hands.'

TANYA. Of course. You always look at their hands.

VICTOR. 'Look at their hands', yeah?

TANYA. The callouses, the scars, the rings, the thickness of the fingers, the tenderness. Get up, Vitya, please.

VICTOR. So, I looked at their hands.

Was there care in their hands? Didn't look at their faces, only their hands. Was there care in their hands? Look at my hands, now.

They are bloody.

These are not my hands.

She holds his hands.

TANYA. Come on – it's time to go.

VICTOR. Where?

TANYA. Don't ask questions

VICTOR. Okay. As simple as that.

They walk through the glass doors. The fire glows.

Blackout.

The End.

A Nick Hern Book

Fast Labour first published in Great Britain in 2008 as a paperback original by Nick Hern Books Limited, 14 Larden Road, London W3 7ST, in association with Hampstead Theatre, London and the West Yorkshire Playhouse, Leeds

Cover image: Photograph of Craig Kelly by Richard Moran. Designed by West Yorkshire Playhouse
Cover design: Ned Hoste, 2H

Typeset by Nick Hern Books, London
Printed in the UK by CPI Antony Rowe, Chippenham, Wiltshire

A CIP catalogue record for this book is available from the British Library

ISBN 978 1 85459 574 4